What reade
The Chris

MW00424351

"This book is a game-changer. Anyone with the desire to make Christ the center of his or her life and home should start with this book. You'll find stories and ideas that are simple to follow and very applicable to everyday life." (Chauntelle B.)

"Emily's words always speak to my soul, and *Creating a Christ-Centered Home* was no different. Emily has a way of understanding scriptures and conveying personal stories that allows the Spirit to open your heart and mind. I am ready for my family to take this journey so Christ can be the center of our home." (Amy C.)

"Reading this book has given me motivation to change things in my home that would make the Savior feel more welcome if He were a guest. The questions posed throughout the book allowed me to measure where I am in my journey to have a more Christ-centered home and what changes need to be made. I look forward to reading this book over and over throughout the years!" (Hailey W.)

"I am so excited to implement the monthly ideas in my home each month. Emily Freeman's ideas on creating a Christ-centered home can help my family and yours." (Laura R.)

"Emily Freeman has selected several favorite stories of Jesus and organized them into a framework that will enable readers to readily place Him at the center of their homes. I look forward to returning to Emily's insights over the coming months to strengthen my relationships both with Jesus and with the members of my family." (Alison W.)

"This book had me hooked from the introduction. As I read it, the warmth and light I felt was so palpable. I came away with a renewed desire that our home would always be a place where the Savior would be comfortable and that those who come and go would feel His love for them." (Connie G.)

"*Creating a Christ-Centered Home* provides the perfect blueprint for achieving this vital goal. Whether your family consists of several members or you are single, the ideas and suggestions in this book will change your home!" (Beth M.)

"This book has the power to change lives. I look forward to applying the principles knowing that the atmosphere of our home will change and our hearts will be filled with Christ-like love." (Brittany A.)

"In *Creating a Christ-Centered Home*, Emily Freeman helps us apply what we are learning about Christ by inviting us to take action. This book invites us to reach even more of our potential, live with intention, and create a fun learning environment along the way." (Marisa S.)

THE
Christ-Centered
HOME

THE
Christ-Centered
HOME

Inviting Jesus In

EMILY BELLE FREEMAN

ENSIGN
PEAK

Art direction by Richard Erickson
Design by Sheryl Dickert Smith and Barry Hansen
Book design © 2016 Ensign Peak

Cover image © Annotee/Shutterstock.com
Border around interior door photos © jadimages/Shutterstock.com
Interior door photos: page x © Iryna_Kolesova/Shutterstock.com; page 8 © villorejo/
Shutterstock.com; page 18 © HUANG Zheng/Shutterstock.com; page 34 © Eugene
Sergeev/Shutterstock.com; page 46 © LacoKozyna/Shutterstock.com; page 60 ©
maurizio/Shutterstock.com; page 74 © Francesco Maltinti/Shutterstock.com; page 90
© Byjeng/Shutterstock.com; page 102 © Veronika Galkina/Shutterstock.com; page 114
© Nuttawut Uttamaharad/Shutterstock.com; page 128 © Romas_Photo/Shutterstock.
com; page 140 © Laborant/Shutterstock.com; page 152 © mikhail/Shutterstock.com

Visit us at EnsignPeakPublishing.com

Library of Congress Cataloging-in-Publication Data
Names: Freeman, Emily, 1969– author.
Title: The Christ-centered home : inviting Jesus in / Emily Belle Freeman.
Description: Salt Lake City, Utah : Ensign Peak, [2016] | ?2016 | Includes bibliographical
    references.
Identifiers: LCCN 2015037587 | ISBN 9781629721552 (paperbound)
Subjects: LCSH: Christian life.
Classification: LCC BV4501.3 .F73928 2016 | DDC 248.4—dc23
LC record available at http://lccn.loc.gov/2015037587

Printed in the United States of America
Edwards Brothers Malloy, Ann Arbor, MI

10 9 8 7 6 5 4 3 2 1

For
Caleb and Maria,
Josh and Janaye,
J.J. and Meg,
and Garett and Natalie,
. . . four weddings in less than one year . . .
this is my wish for you.

CONTENTS

CONTENTS

IN EVERY HOUSE,
THEY CEASED NOT
TO TEACH AND PREACH
JESUS CHRIST.

Acts 5:42

AN INTRODUCTION

Every so often, the whole sky comes crashing down. That was the case recently for a dear friend of mine who unexpectedly found out that his two-year-old daughter, Hope, had cancer. Life has a peculiar way of marching forward after a shattering moment like that. The sun still rises, breakfast still has to be served, and diapers still need to be changed.

Somewhere in the middle of chemotherapy and hospital stays and IV tubes, my friend and his daughter had a conversation familiar to everyone who has raised a young child. It had been a long day, and my friend held Hope in his arms as he read her a bedtime story. In his silliest voice he asked, "What does the owl say?"

Hope replied, "Whoo, whoo!" She giggled sweetly, and he couldn't help but notice how much hair she had lost in the past few days. Patchy and brittle, her remaining strawberry blonde wisps were a painful reminder of the reality of their situation.

My friend turned the page and asked, "What does the cow say?"

"Moo, moo!" Hope responded proudly and grinned from ear to ear. The little wisps of hair that had fallen in her lap as they were reading didn't seem to bother her at all. My friend looked up to read the next line, and suddenly the conversation took an unexpected turn. At that moment, a picture of Jesus on Hope's bedroom wall caught his attention, and he asked an unplanned question.

"Hopie," he stammered, trying not to give away his emotion, "What does Jesus say?" It was a question he had never asked her before.

As he waited with anticipation, Hope snuggled into his shoulder, opened wide her big blue eyes, and whispered, "Hold you. Jesus say, 'Hold you.'" My friend burst into tears. He gently pulled his daughter's little body into his and hugged her as he sobbed deep, heavy sobs. A few minutes later, he held her up to the light switch so she could turn off her bedroom lamp. After Hope said good night to the trees in the front yard and a blue glass star that hung in her window, he set her gently into her crib with her blanket that had been soaked through with his tears. As he walked quietly out of her room, he reflected on the lesson he had just been taught and the gentle reminder he had been given that Jesus was holding their family in His loving arms.

On that unforgettable night, a picture of Jesus that had been hung on the wall of Hope's room prepared the way for a profound lesson to be taught. In a place where everyday routine collided with heaven's truth, sweet peace filled up heavy hearts. Christ became the center of the conversation, and in that still moment, an added measure of strength was found, hearts were lifted, and courage was renewed.

So it is every time we turn to Jesus Christ.

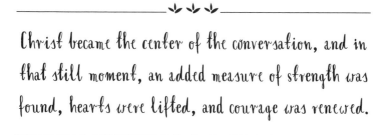

Christ became the center of the conversation, and in that still moment, an added measure of strength was found, hearts were lifted, and courage was renewed.

In my mind I keep going back to that evening. At some point beforehand, my friend had chosen to hang that picture in his daughter's room. My guess is that it was months before, in a time of joy. I assume that he had no idea of the strength the picture would bring in a future moment of need.

This experience reaffirmed a truth that I believe with my whole heart: there is a great power that comes when Jesus Christ becomes the central focus of our home. If our conversations center on Christ, if pictures of Him hang on our walls, if His words have a place in our hearts, and if His attributes become characteristics of each member of our family, we will experience an added measure of peace, strength, courage, and hope in the moments when we need it most. But how is it done?

I spent a lot of time pondering that question over the

past year. It was late one evening when the answer finally came. *What better way to learn about having a Christ-centered home than from Christ Himself?* What if we turned to the New Testament and focused on the lessons Jesus taught within the walls of the actual homes of His followers? Would those lessons help us make Jesus the focal point of our own homes?

After that epiphany, I completely immersed myself in the accounts of the four Gospels. I read specifically looking for the time Jesus spent inside people's homes. As I began to study the lessons that Jesus taught in the homes of His followers, I started taking notes of the things I wanted to remember to teach my own family. As I read, I realized that I could be more deliberate in making my home Christ centered. Through this process, twelve lessons stood out to me. They were powerful and yet simple. Looking over the lessons, I wondered what would happen if our family chose to devote one year to studying each one and applying its principles to our own home.

Hence, this twelve-month journey.

Perhaps you would like to join this journey—a journey that is not meant to overwhelm, but rather to simply enrich. Maybe you could set aside one night every month for your family to experience a Christ-centered conversation, connection, and celebration. On this night, your *conversation* could include discussing a lesson Jesus taught within the walls of one of His follower's homes, and then you could set a family goal that would allow your family to *connect* personally with that lesson, and you might want to whip up a fun treat to snack on while you talk about each lesson—this is the *celebration.* Maybe you will hang a print in your home to remind you of the lesson you are trying to work on that month (visit www.christcenteredcelebrations.com for images and reminders you can download and print).

The scriptures contain powerful lessons that have the potential to bring about positive change. I believe these twelve lessons have that potential. Already my heart has begun to anticipate the journey ahead. This year I intend to make time for deliberately planned conversations, connec-

I want to know Him better, seek Him more often, and fill my home with tangible reminders that He is at the center of everything we do.

tions, and celebrations that will focus on Jesus Christ. I long to create settings that will allow my children to personally experience His love. I want to know Him better, seek Him more often, and fill my home with tangible reminders that He is at the center of everything we do.

Every month, as we accompany the Savior into the homes of His followers, I want to ask one simple question—the question my friend asked his daughter as he held her in his arms, the question that will lead to an increase of hope, peace, comfort, strength, and courage:

What does Jesus say?

THE HOUSE OF ZACCHAEUS

A Household Where

He Abides

THE FIRST MONTH

Invite Him In

Have you ever received an invitation to stay at someone's home? Not long ago I accepted such an invitation. I walked into the home after a long flight and sat at the kitchen counter. The aroma from the beautiful home-grown orchids that had been placed in vases surrounding the kitchen sink was enchanting. My hostess and I sat and talked while snacking on plump ruby raspberries, deep purple blackberries, and sweet red strawberries. The conversation was uplifting; we spoke of friendship and how to make deep connections that would sustain in times of trouble and uplift in moments of routine. After our sweet afternoon snack I retired to my room to unpack and unwind—a bit of rest and peace after the whirlwind of travel. It seemed that my hostess knew just what was needed just when I needed it most. I look back on the three days I spent in that home with fond memories of good conversation and gracious care. I left wondering whether my home was as welcoming as hers had been and what I could do to make it more inviting.

Luke chapter 19 begins with a man named Zacchaeus sitting high in the branches of a sycamore tree. Zacchaeus didn't just end up in the tree by chance; he climbed up there on purpose. The streets around him were lined with curious people, the crowds so thick that Zacchaeus was unable to find a spot where he would be able to see the Lord as He walked past. Zacchaeus likely heard people in the crowd saying that Jesus was getting close to the place where he stood, but even standing on the very tips of his toes couldn't help his view, so he ran ahead and climbed up into a sycamore tree to see the Lord.

When Jesus came to the tree He looked up, saw Zacchaeus sitting there in the branches, and said, "Zacchaeus, make haste, and come down; for to day I must abide at thy house" (Luke 19:5). So Zacchaeus came down from the tree and received Jesus into his home joyfully.

Every time I read this story, the same question enters my mind:

If Jesus were to visit my home unexpectedly, would I be prepared to receive Him joyfully?

The lesson Jesus taught within the walls of this home is simple but important. Zacchaeus had no knowledge beforehand that the Lord would be stopping in for a visit that afternoon. And yet he was ready. He was prepared to receive Jesus joyfully. His house stood ready to welcome a guest, but even more important, Zacchaeus was also prepared as a host fit to welcome the Lord into his home.

Would the same be true of you or me?

If Jesus were to visit my home unexpectedly, would I be prepared to receive Him joyfully?

Think about your home for a minute. If Jesus came to your doorstep, **would you be prepared to welcome Him in?**

_____

_____

_____

How about your house? Is it ready to welcome a guest? Consider the pictures that hang on your walls. Think about the items you have placed on your shelves. **Is your home clean and inviting?**

_____

_____

_____

Last, consider the ambiance. How about the conversations that take place within the walls of your home? Are they uplifting? Do people speak kindly? **Would the Lord be comfortable there?**

_____

_____

_____

Pondering these questions led me to develop a great

admiration for Zacchaeus and the fact that he was able to invite the Lord into his home with haste and with great joy. He did not hesitate. He was ready. I hope the same would be true of me.

One of my favorite descriptive verbs in this account is the word *abide*. To abide means to come and stay. It isn't a short visit; it carries with it a sense of lingering. Jesus chose to *abide* at the house of Zacchaeus; He chose to linger there.

A home where Jesus would choose to abide doesn't just happen by chance; it is something we must intentionally create day after day after day.

We do not live in New Testament times, and it won't be our opportunity to have a conversation with the Lord from a sycamore tree—one in which He invites Himself into our homes. But I do love the thought of inviting the *Spirit* of the Lord to abide, to come and stay, to linger in our homes. A home where Jesus would choose to abide doesn't just happen by chance; it is something we must intentionally create day after day after day.

One of the ways we can prepare to invite the Spirit into our homes is to look carefully at what we might learn from the admonition of Paul: "Whatsoever things are true, whatsoever things are honest, whatsoever things are just, whatsoever things are pure, whatsoever things are lovely, whatsoever things are of good report; if there be any virtue, and if there be any praise, think on these things" (Philippians 4:8).

Think for a moment of your home. Do words like *true, honorable, just, pure, lovely, commendable, excellent,* or *worthy of praise* come to mind? Take a minute to reflect on the rooms where your family spends the most time. Now, think of each of those words. Is there anything you would take away, add, or change in some way to make your home more prepared for the Spirit of the Lord to abide there? Paintings of the Savior, scripture verses on the wall, and uplifting quotes or prints can all bring a sweet spirit into our homes. **What other ideas do these words from Philippians inspire?**

_____

_____

_____

The lesson Jesus taught in Zacchaeus' home is just as important today as it was in New Testament times. We must not hesitate to invite the Spirit of the Lord into our homes. Instead, we should take care every day to prepare our homes so that the Spirit of the Lord can abide there. The promise of Zacchaeus' story is that our ongoing preparations to invite the Spirit of the Lord to abide, to come and stay, to linger, will bring us moments of great joy.

Invite Him In

THE CONVERSATION

Luke 19:1–10

Spend some time together reflecting on the story of Zacchaeus. There are three important lessons we learn from his story. First, to make haste rather than hesitate as we prepare our homes to receive the Spirit of the Lord. Second, to be ready always to recognize the Spirit of the Lord. Last, to receive that Spirit joyfully and allow Him to abide within our homes.

THE CONNECTION

After your conversation, choose one way your family could prepare to invite the Spirit of the Lord to abide in your home for this whole month. Write down your goal and hang it somewhere in your home as a reminder.

_____

_____

_____

THE CELEBRATION

Shelly's Chex Mix

Mix together in large bowl:

> ½ large box each of Corn Chex, Rice Chex,
> and Golden Grahams
> ¾ cup shredded coconut
> 1¾ cups sliced almonds

Boil:

> 2 cups light corn syrup
> 2 cups sugar
> 1½ cups butter

Pour syrup over dry mix and stir. Spread on a cookie sheet and cover for one hour.

Consider preparing the mix ahead of time so it is ready when your discussion begins. Then you can nibble as you talk.

THE LESSON FROM
THE HOUSE OF ZACCHAEUS

🌿 🌿 🌿

If you seek a household where Jesus abides, invite Him in.

THE HOUSE ON THE BORDERS OF TYRE

A Household of

Faith

THE SECOND MONTH

Expect Miracles

When I was young, my mother would often make homemade wheat bread. Those hot summer afternoons are filled with tangible memories for me—the grinding of the wheat into powder, the kneading of the warm dough, the waiting and watching for the loaf to rise. After the process was complete, after the baking and the shaking out of tin pans and the slicing, there was the butter lathered onto the steaming slice of bread, topped off with a spoonful of raspberry jam. Some memories are so much more than just photographs—they come with sweet smells, vivid touch, and lingering taste. This memory is one of those.

Sometimes, when I read the New Testament, I feel as if the memory of a mother making bread must have stirred the heartstrings of those who listened to Jesus. Perhaps it is one reason why Jesus loved to use bread as a symbol in His teachings. But there is a deeper reason for this simple object lesson. For believers, bread represents more than just a warm treat on a summer afternoon. It leads our thoughts to the Last Supper, to the Bread of Life, to Jesus Christ. I have learned to pay close attention when bread is introduced in a chapter of the scriptures; I know that I am about to learn more about Jesus.

Such is the case in Mark 7. The story I want to share with you is bookended on either side by stories about bread. The chapter begins with a heated debate over whether or not the disciples washed their hands before eating the bread they had been given. The chapter that follows recounts the miracle of feeding the four thousand, with seven baskets full of bread remaining. Right in the middle of these verses we read a story about crumbs.

After the argument about the bread, Jesus left and journeyed into the borders of Tyre and Sidon. He left Galilee behind and traveled into the Gentile regions, stopping to rest inside a home, hoping that no one would notice, "but he could not be hid" (Mark 7:24).

It was in this home that a certain woman found him—a woman whose daughter was severely oppressed by a demon. Somehow this woman, who was not of the Jewish faith, had heard of Jesus. We do not know much about this woman, but one thing is made clear by her actions: this gentile woman had a heart that contained a seed of faith. When she entered the home, she came and fell at the feet of Jesus. It is not hard to imagine this mother exhausted from caring for her daughter. We picture the burden weighing heavy on her shoulders and the worry written into the lines of her face. When I envision that mother bent over at the feet of Jesus, there is only one thought that comes to mind: humble surrender.

Jesus must have seen the exhaustion, the weight, the worry. He must have sensed the longing. But He had to be certain of the intent of the woman's heart. Speaking directly to her, He explained that it was not right to take the bread of the children and feed it to the dogs.

Maybe our first inclination is to think His comment rude. But that would not be consistent with what we know about Jesus.

Perhaps, instead, He was questioning the woman's alignment, giving her time to process the desire held deep within her heart and to tie it to the seed of faith that would lead her to believe in Him. Her answer was immediate: "Yes, Lord: yet the dogs under the table eat of the children's crumbs." *I want to experience the bread, Your bread, so deeply that I will take whatever you will give me.*

Give me even the crumbs.

When I consider the desire in my heart and my willingness to believe in the Lord, how often is my response, I will take whatever you will give me? How much do I want what only the Lord can give?

I can't help but pause here and wonder if my response would have been the same. When I consider the desire in my heart and my willingness to believe in the Lord, how often is my response, *I will take whatever you will give me?* How much do I want what only the Lord can give?

His response to this mother was immediate: "O woman, great is thy faith: be it unto thee even as thou wilt" (Matthew 15:28). He gave her more than a crumb; He gave her a miracle. That is the way of the Lord. One thing I love most about this woman is that she approached the Lord expecting a miracle. That is not my nature. I don't know whether it is a lack of faith or an unnecessary attempt to settle for something less, but rarely do I enter a situation with as much faith and expectation as this woman did. It is a weakness of mine.

He gave her more than a crumb;
He gave her a miracle.
That is the way of the Lord.

Several years ago I found a magnet that I keep on my refrigerator. It says, "Expect Miracles." Two simple words that remind me of this humble woman's faith. For me, the story taught in this home on the borders of Tyre becomes a lesson on desire, on faith, and on the miracles that follow humble belief in Him.

In Titus we read the counsel to "set in order the things that are wanting" (Titus 1:5).

Take a few minutes to think about this. What are the things that are wanting in your home? What are the most pressing needs? What is it that weighs heavy on your shoulders? What fills your heart with worry? **Where is your desire?**

Perhaps it is not a burden that you carry. Maybe instead you feel desire in the form of something you lack. It might be that you long for more peace in your home. Or contentment. Or joy. Discovering our desire leads us to moments of true reflection.

Following the pattern shown in the home this woman visited will help us individually and as families to turn to the Lord in faith, with the belief that He can satisfy our true desire. There are several lessons we learn from this mother: she *heard* of the Lord, and *came,* and *fell* at His feet. Consider how these three actions might lead to an increase of faith.

First, to *hear*. **Where are the places you turn to hear of the Lord?** Scriptures, worship music, and trusted leaders come to mind. How often do those opportunities to hear of the Lord take place within the walls of your home?

The next step of faith required this woman to *come* to Him. What does that look like in your life? Perhaps prayer, meditation, and reflection are ways for you to come to Him. **Where are the holy places you and your family visit that lead you closer to Him?** Would you consider your home to be one of those holy places? What might you need to adjust to create that kind of sanctuary?

_____

_____

_____

The last action of this woman expresses an important principle about faith. She understood that more than just hearing and coming would be required—true faith included the sincerest form of worship: humble surrender. She *fell down* and placed her desire at the feet of the Lord. Are we willing to do the same?

Are you willing to fall at His feet in humble surrender? To ask for what only He can give? **What would this type of worship look like?**

_____

_____

_____

On a regular basis, time and time again, we must make this decision. Through the lifelong process of hearing of Him and coming closer to Him, we must take the time to determine again our alignment, to reaffirm our willingness to believe.

I was seventeen weeks pregnant when I went into labor with my youngest daughter. In an effort to save the pregnancy

I was put on bed rest, where I remained for the next six months. At night I rested in my bed, during the day I rested on the couch, and for ten minutes every evening I was allowed to sit in a lawn chair in my front yard. My only excursion every week was a trip to the doctor's office. It wasn't long before I became discouraged with my situation. To make matters worse, at every doctor's visit, my doctor would remind me of the reality of the situation I was in by gently telling me that he wasn't sure we would get a healthy baby at the end of the ordeal. "Things are just too volatile," he said. "I just don't know if you will even make it through the next week."

I was relying on my own strength to make it through, but I needed to rely on the Lord's strength.

There was a day when I felt I could not do it any longer. It seemed every muscle of my body was taut with the effort of trying to hold the baby in. I was exhausted. I remember telling Greg that I was finished; I was giving up on trying to reach full term. I will never forget his reply: "I have never seen you like this. Where is your faith? I don't remember a time when you haven't held on to faith." It was the reminder I needed. I was relying on my own strength to make it through, but I needed to rely on the Lord's strength.

On the afternoon when Grace was born, several nurses gathered around my bed to prepare for the delivery. The doctor lifted her up just after she was born so we could all see her long, blonde hair. "Take a good look at this baby," he said to the nurses. "This is a miracle baby. She would not be here if it were not for the faith of her mother."

My mind immediately flashed back to the day when Greg had gently reminded me to hold on to my faith. I realized in that moment that through the hardship of that trial I had come to know the Lord in a very personal way. I had learned what it meant to come to Him and to fall at His feet. I had turned my burden over to Him with the decision to live in faith, and because of that choice I had been blessed to experience a miracle.

Life has a way of questioning the intention of our heart. Daily we are faced with choices that either increase or tear down faith. Think back over the last twenty-four hours. How many of the minutes that filled those hours were filled with actions that would lead to an increase of faith?

At the root of this woman's miracle we discover the very essence of faith. We see in her an assurance of faith. Faith is what allowed the blessing to come. In one of the most defining moments of her life, this woman responded with faith—first. Would we? Would our children?

What would it take to create a home in which we choose faith first? Before self-sufficiency, before common sense, before practicality? Would life be different if the most important characteristic of our dwelling was that it was known as a household of faith? What would that kind of home look like?

Hebrews chapter 11 contains one of the most powerful definitions of what faith looks like. It includes both the guiding principles of faith along with the blessings or promises that follow faith.

Guiding Principles

By faith we offer God our righteousness.

By faith we draw near to God.

By faith we obey.

By faith we are able to stand strong with the people of God.

By faith we endure.

By faith we keep God's commandments.

By faith we rise again to a better life.

We live by faith.

Take some time with your family to talk about that list. Do those guiding principles have a place in your home? Could you make a list of what those principles look like in your daily actions? Is yours a household of faith? (see Galatians 6:10).

_____

_____

_____

Now consider some of the promises that follow faith as found in Hebrews 11.

Promises

> By faith we understand.
>
> By faith we are warned.
>
> By faith we receive strength beyond our own.
>
> By faith we are blessed.
>
> By faith the obstacles we face fall down.
>
> By faith we conquer, obtain promises, stop harm, escape, are made strong out of weakness, and become mighty.

Take a few minutes to look through this list. **What blessings have come to your family through faith?**

_____

_____

_____

The next chapter of Hebrews continues this lesson of faith. Hebrews 12 explains that it is through faith that we are able to set aside every weight as we look unto Jesus, who perfects our faith. Just like the woman in this house, we can look to Jesus and we, too, can set aside our weight. Every weight. And, in the moments when our faith feels insufficient, He will perfect it. We only need to follow the admonition to "consider Him" (Hebrews 12:3).

A home that is founded on faith is a home in which Jesus Christ is considered daily. A home where His voice can be heard. A home where all are invited to come unto

Him. A home filled with humble surrender and desire for what only He can give. A home where people turn to Jesus first—in faith. A home filled with people who know that life would be benefited by even crumbs, but who are blessed instead with miracles.

Expect Miracles

THE CONVERSATION
Mark 7:24–30

What are the things that are wanting in your home? What blessing do you seek from the Lord? How could you approach that need by responding with faith first? Look back at the list of guiding principles from Hebrews 11. Which principles are found in your home? Are there some that might need more focus? Discuss the blessings that follow faith. Has your family been privileged to experience any of those?

THE CONNECTION

If we choose to live by faith we must open our eyes to see God's miracles, because the two go hand in hand. Hang a poster in a prominent place in your home. Write the words *Expect Miracles* across the top. Try to live in faith with humble expectation every day. Write on the poster the miracles that take place in your home throughout this month.

THE CELEBRATION

Raspberry Honey Butter

Mix: ¾ cup softened butter
¼ cup honey
½ cup raspberry jam
1 teaspoon vanilla

Spread on top of baked rolls fresh out of the oven.

Consider adding 1 teaspoon of cinnamon instead of the raspberry jam for a yummy fall spread.

THE LESSON FROM THE HOUSE ON THE BORDERS OF TYRE

———————— ⚜ ⚜ ⚜ ————————

If you seek a household of faith, expect miracles.

THE HOUSE IN GALILEE

A Household of

Prayer

THE THIRD MONTH

Converse with Him

I t was one man in the midst of the multitude—a man who came seeking a blessing for a boy who was beyond hope. The trial weighed heavy on both father and son, so heavy that the father came seeking for the compassion of the Lord. "If thou canst do any thing," he begged. Jesus replied, "If thou canst believe, all things are possible to him that believeth." Immediately, "The father of the child cried out, and said with tears, Lord, I believe; help thou mine unbelief" (Mark 9:17–24). Then Jesus rebuked the spirit, and took the young boy by the hand, and lifted him up.

It was just after this miracle, when Jesus had come into the house in Galilee, that His disciples asked Him in private why they could not heal the boy. His reply was simple, but important: "This kind can come forth by nothing, but by prayer and fasting" (Mark 9:29). In this home an important lesson about the power of prayer was taught. When someone in our home requires a blessing from the Lord, our prayers in their behalf can become a powerful source for good. Prayer can lead to miracles.

Consider the prayer habits of your family. How often do you pray for the members of your family? Do you mention them by name?

Abraham Lincoln learned this powerful lesson from his own mother. He reportedly said, "I remember my mother's prayers and they have always followed me. They have clung to me all my life." His mother must have been a mother who prayed powerful prayers. Oh, how I wish that my prayers would follow my children. I love that he said his mother's prayers *clung* to him, as if he could not be separated from them. What great comfort that must have brought him. But just holding on to his mother's prayers was not enough. Lincoln learned that he, too, could have a relationship with the Lord. "I have been driven many times upon my knees by the overwhelming conviction that I had nowhere else to go. My own wisdom and that of all about me seemed insufficient for that day." His mother left him with more than just prayers that clung to him; she gave him a powerful resource, a knowledge of how he could personally speak with God.

One of our sons is a junior college football player. He has a lot of talent, and that talent has given him the opportunity to receive offers to play for many different colleges across the United States. As part of the recruiting process, it has been my privilege to speak on the telephone with head coaches from all over the country. I am surprised how many of them are men of God. These are churchgoing coaches, most of them. And they are raising more than just football players—they are raising honorable men. Sure, we talk about scholarships, and positions, and play time. But more importantly, we talk of morals, and attending church, and Jesus.

I don't know a whole lot about football. But I know about Jesus.

A few weeks ago I had the opportunity to talk to the head coach of Arizona State University, Todd Graham. There is a part of that conversation that I won't ever forget as long as I live. It was when Coach Graham told me about his mom. He spoke of how she raised him, what he learned from her, and how she prayed for him several times a day. "She spoke victory over us," he explained. I stopped dead in my tracks in that moment and started searching for a pen and a scrap of paper. I had to write it down. It was a phrase I didn't ever want to forget.

Speak victory.

—Todd Graham

The image of a mother speaking victory over her son several times a day penetrated deep down into my heart. I want to be a mom like that. I want to keep regular appointments with God to discuss each of my children. I want to speak victory over them. You might have thought I would have learned something about football from a man like Coach Graham. Instead, we spoke of the kind of victories that can only be won through Jesus. Victories that come through prayer.

If you want your home to be more Christ centered, let it become a house of prayer. As you study this topic this month, prepare to share your feelings about prayer with your family. Mention your family members by name when they hear you pray. When they approach you for help or advice, consider asking them if they have thought to include the Lord. Maybe you will spend an evening sharing times in your life when you have received answers to prayers. Ask members of your family to share the times when they have received an answer or comfort or strength through prayer. **What are some of the experiences in your life that have deepened your desire to live more prayerfully?**

When we teach our children to rely on the power of prayer, it will become a source of strength that they will carry throughout all the days of their lives.

I won't forget the moment when Jesus reinforced the importance of prayer in the temple. "And Jesus went into the temple of God, and cast out all them that sold and bought in the temple, and overthrew the tables of the moneychangers, and the seats of them that sold doves, and said unto them, It is written, My house shall be called the house of prayer" (Matthew 21:12–13). The reason behind the Lord's actions was to restore the temple to its highest function, which was to serve as a house of prayer. The temple, central to Jewish religious life, was meant to lead people to the true worship of God, with prayer being one of the highest forms of worship. Just like we saw Jesus do in the temple, we might need to set aside or overturn some things to make prayer a priority in our lives.

How might this be true in your home?

_____

_____

_____

A true relationship with Jesus begins through conversations with Him. In our home we talk about this on a regular basis. Consider your very best friend. How often do you talk to that person? Daily? How many times daily? What would happen if you didn't talk to that friend at all this week? What if you avoided them all month? What would happen to your relationship then? Just as is true with our close friends, daily conversations are central to developing a relationship with Jesus Christ.

But that can be hard, especially if prayer doesn't currently fall into the normal routine of our day.

Many years ago I made a conscious decision to include the Lord in the daily conversation of my life. Rather than limiting myself to a morning and evening prayer or prayers at mealtimes, I decided to include Him in the daily walk of my life. If the sunrise was beautiful, I paused to let Him know. If I was struggling with a customer service representative on an irritating phone call, I offered up a quick prayer that I might know the words to say. When I got in the car for a twenty-minute drive, I turned off the radio and filled Him in on the events of the day. In moments of need, I turned to Him first. In moments of gratitude, I stopped to rejoice heavenward. His was the last conversation I had before my eyes closed and the first conversation I entered into as the day began.

That decision changed my life. It has changed the way I view my relationship with the Lord, and it has allowed me to see His hand more clearly in the ordinary events of my day. Because I invited Him to be such an integral part, He has blessed my life beyond measure. Now I can't get through the day without talking with Him several times. *He* has become the pattern of my day.

Prayer is the last conversation I have before my eyes close and the first conversation I enter into as the day begins.

Making prayer a part of our daily routine may require us to set aside and turn upside down many of our original daily patterns. We have to shift our thoughts vertically. Inviting the Lord to be part of our lives will require us to live intentionally. But the blessing of constant companionship is worth it. The ongoing conversation will bless our lives in a way that we may have been missing out on previously. Through prayer we can receive answers, comfort, and strength. We can experience the miracles that can come only through prayer and fasting. We can find direction. Perhaps the most important lesson we can teach our children is the importance of regular prayer.

Converse with Him

THE CONVERSATION
Mark 9:17–24

Have you ever wanted a blessing from the Lord for someone who is dear to you? Did you pray by name in behalf of that person? Can you think of a time when your prayers for another person have been answered?

THE CONNECTION

Consider setting a goal to pray for specific family members this month. Remember to mention them by name. I have a friend who keeps a prayer list on her nightstand. As she thinks back on each day, she adds names of the people she knows who need a blessing from the Lord. What is something you could do to remember to pray for each individual in your home?

THE CELEBRATION

Grandma Leslie's Popcorn

Boil until barely at soft ball stage:

> ¾ cup brown sugar
> ¾ cup cane sugar
> ½ cup light corn syrup
> ½ cup water
> ⅛ teaspoon cream of tartar
> 1½ cups butter

As soon as you hit the soft ball stage, add:

> 1 teaspoon baking soda
> 1 teaspoon vanilla

Pour over 6 cups of popped popcorn.

The fun part about this recipe is watching the syrup bubble up when you add the baking soda. Your kids will love it. Make sure the pan is large enough for the syrup to rise.

THE LESSON FROM
THE HOUSE IN GALILEE

🌿 🌿 🌿

If you seek a household of prayer, converse with Him.

THE HOUSE OF JAIRUS

A Household of

Scripture

THE FOURTH MONTH
Embrace the Stories of Jesus

He was at lunch when a certain ruler, Jairus, approached the place where He sat. Falling at His feet, the humble man begged Jesus to come to his home, "for he had one only daughter, about twelve years of age, and she lay dying" (Luke 8:42).

With Jairus in the lead, they made their way down a very busy street. During a brief pause, Jesus stopped to heal a woman who had reached out to touch His robe, and then the journey resumed. Suddenly, one came with news from the ruler's house: "Thy daughter is dead; trouble not the Master. But when Jesus heard it, he answered him, saying, Fear not: believe only" (Luke 8:49–50).

It wasn't long before they came to the house. As they approached, they could see the tumult and hear the cacophony of those who wept within. Upon entering the home, Jesus addressed the tumult first. He questioned the intentions of those who were mourning. They laughed at His assurance of faith. He must have explained that there was no reason for the mourning to continue; Jesus did not want the tumult, the mourning, or the mocking to linger. In an effort to prepare the home for what was about to take place, He "put them all out" (Mark 5:40). He removed the distraction.

Within the hush that surely followed, a small group entered the room where the young girl lay. There, within the peace, the Savior stretched out His hand, and taking the girl's tiny hand in His, bid her to arise. It is not hard to picture that moment of reunion and rejoicing, a mother scooping her daughter up into her arms, a father drawing in a quick breath of astonishment, the disciples caught up

There is a humility that comes when we invite the Lord into our most private spaces. Within that hush we hear the gentle whisper of His voice, we see His hand, we feel the prompting to rise.

in wonder. The parting advice from the Lord was simple, and yet compelling: "Give her meat" (Luke 8:55). For this young girl, who had required healing that only a miracle could bring, what was needed now was meat. Sustenance. A life-giving source that would give her strength.

Sometimes when I read this account, I consider a figurative application for our day. I picture a father consumed with worry over a daughter who is struggling spiritually. I can imagine him petitioning the Lord, asking for His help with the heavy burden weighing on his shoulders. Perhaps

there is preparation that needs to take place in the home before the blessing can come. Quieting the tumult. Removing
the distractions. A preparation for the healing that he seeks.
I imagine a mother and father extending an invitation for
the Lord to enter the innermost parts of their home. There
is a humility that comes when we invite the Lord into our
most private spaces. Within that hush we hear the gentle
whisper of His voice, we see His hand, we feel the prompting to rise. Perhaps, when all is said and done, the counsel
to this figurative father would be similar to the advice given
to Jairus in regard to his young daughter. Give her meat.
Sustenance. Give her a life-giving source that will give her
strength, something that will help her survive spiritually.
Perhaps this life-giving source, this sustenance, this spiritual
meat, could be found within the pages of scripture.

It was shortly after this miracle took place that Jesus
asked the disciples who they thought He was. Peter answered immediately, "Thou art the Christ" (Mark 8:29).
The disciples had witnessed the miracle of Jairus' daughter, the feeding of 5,000, the healing of the blind. "It was
through what He did . . . that they learned who He was"
(Alfred Edersheim, *The Life and Times of Jesus the Messiah*
[Peabody, Massachusetts: Hendrickson Publisher, 1993],
924). I imagine the same is true for us. By reading what
Jesus did in the pages of the New Testament, we come to
know for ourselves who He was. The stories become for us
sustenance, spiritual meat, a source of strength.

That meat is available not only to us, but is also something we can give to our children. It will require removing

distractions, calming the tumult, preparing for moments of quiet that will allow us to invite Him in as we immerse ourselves and our family in His word.

What are some ways you can remove the distractions and calm the tumult in your own home?

For most children, spiritual education begins in the home. It has always been so, even in the homes of the earliest recorded scripture. Alfred Edersheim explains how a young Jewish child would begin learning religious devotion from an early age by watching his or her mother. He speaks of the religious duties that were placed exclusively upon these mothers: "The Sabbath meal, the kindling of the Sabbath lamp, and the setting apart a portion of the dough from the bread for the household,—these are but instances, with which every 'Taph,' as he clung to his mother's skirts, must have been familiar. Even before he could follow her in such religious household duties, his eyes must have been attracted to the Mezuzah attached to the doorpost, as the name of the Most High on the outside of the little folded parchment was reverently touched by each who came or went. . . . It was the symbol of the Divine guard over Israel's homes, the visible emblem of this joyous hymn: 'The Lord shall preserve thy going out and coming in, from this time forth, and even for evermore'" (Edersheim, *Life and Times of Jesus*, 642).

Affixed to the door of some Jewish homes you will find a mezuzah, a piece of parchment inscribed with verses from Deuteronomy. These verses compose the Jewish prayer "Shema Yisrael." The parchment is usually kept in a decorative case and fulfills the Biblical commandment to inscribe the words of the Shema on the doorposts of your home.

I discovered these verses in Deuteronomy when I was a young mother. They have had a profound influence on how I have mothered my children. They impressed upon me a great desire to use the scriptures frequently in my home. "And these words . . . shall be in thine heart: And thou shalt teach them diligently unto thy children, and shalt talk of them when thou sittest in thine house, and when thou walkest by the way, and when thou liest down, and when thou risest up . . . and thou shalt write them upon the posts of thy house, and on thy gates" (Deuteronomy 6:6–9). The words of this prayer, which continue in Deuteronomy 11, counsel us to love the Lord, to take heed that our heart be not deceived, and to lay up the Lord's words in our heart and in our soul (see Deuteronomy 11:13–21).

I find myself filled with holy envy for this mezuzah, this reminder to cherish the word of the Lord. Often the case of the mezuzah is tilted so that the top slants toward the room into which the door opens. It implies that God and His word are entering the room. The symbolism is powerful—it is a reminder that God and His word stand guard over Israel's homes.

I can't help but wonder if the same is true of my home. Does God's word stand guard over my children? over my family? over my home?

If you could choose a scripture to hang over the door of your home, what would it be?

_____

_____

_____

The question has led me to reflect on how I might incorporate scripture more deeply into the fundamental practices and daily disciplines of my home.

The verses in Deuteronomy suggest that our intent must be accompanied by action. We can't just wish for the words to be in our heart. Rather, we must take action to help the words find a place within our hearts. These actions include teaching the scriptures in our home, talking about them as we gather together, reading them before we lie down and again when we rise up, and putting reminders of the words on display in our homes.

As you consider these ideas, perhaps you will notice areas where your family has already invited the words into your hearts. Maybe these suggestions give you an idea for an area or two where you might improve. Over the years, I have collected advice on how to help the scriptures become an integral part of the daily patterns of our home life. Here are some of our favorites:

- Ask each child what his or her favorite scripture story is. Find a picture depicting that story and hang it in the child's room.

- Have your children draw pictures of the scripture story taking place as you read it to them.

- Read scriptures together every night before bed or every morning at breakfast.

- As children get older, help them learn how to immerse themselves in personal scripture study by gathering together in the same room but having each person read silently for fifteen minutes. Then go around in a circle at the end and have each person share something he or she read.

- Schedule a family walk, and stop for a snack break at various intervals. While you are gathered for a break, share a passage of scripture. Discuss that scripture until you arrive at your next stop.

- Choose a scripture verse to memorize each month, and post it somewhere everyone in your family can see it.

- Encourage each member of your family to keep a personal record of the things he or she is learning in a scripture study journal. Remember to share from the journals.

- Decorate your home with favorite scripture verses.

- Study the scriptures with a question in mind or by a specific topic.

What other scripture study ideas do you have?

_____

_____

_____

The stories of Jesus bring hope, courage, comfort, direction, answers, and insight. As we allow the words of the scriptures to fill our homes, they will become spiritual meat for our children and a source of strength. The scriptures can also become a powerful source of protection as we invite God and His word to stand guard over our homes.

When my children were very young, I made a conscious decision to read from the scriptures every single day. It was a decision that was hard to follow through on, but one that I was adamant about accomplishing. There were a couple of habits that I developed that helped me to fulfill this goal amid the craziness of raising small children. One was that at all times, I left my scriptures open to the place where I was reading. Then I would carry them around from room to room, to the places where I spent most of my time, so that if there was ever a moment of pause I could read a verse or

The scriptures can become a powerful source of protection as we invite God and His word to stand guard over our homes.

two in order to fulfill my goal. At the end of each day you might discover my scriptures on top of the dryer or on the kitchen counter or on the cabinet next to the TV. They were always open and waiting with a red pen nestled in the center in case I found a verse that would give counsel, direction, or guidance for my life. As my reading dedication increased, I found something remarkable happening: my soul longed for the word of the Lord. Often, as I settled into my covers late at night, I would bring my scriptures with me. During that quiet pause at the end of the day, I would reflect on what I had read or take time for a more in-depth study of something I had come across. It was a time of peace at the end of the cacophony of the day.

I hadn't realized that my children were watching all those years. Not until one night when my youngest daughter came and sat on my bed. "I want to do what you do, Mom," she said hesitantly. "I want to read like you do every night before I go to bed. How do I know what to read?" I suggested she start with the New Testament, the stories of Jesus. I knew those words would capture her heart best. It took her a year to finish. She was eleven years old. That was the year she developed a love for reading His word. It has been five years since then, and she still reads her scriptures every single night. Most days end with me going down to the basement to turn out the lights and Grace curled up in her comforter reading the stories of Jesus. As I make my way up the stairs, my mama heart is content with the thought that God and His word are standing guard over her.

Embrace the Stories of Jesus

THE CONVERSATION
Luke 8:41–55

What stands out to you about the healing of Jairus' daughter? Is it the quieting of the house? The removing of the distractions? The mother and father allowing Jesus into the most intimate parts of their home? Why do you think the counsel to "give her meat" could apply to the scriptures? What are some ways you are incorporating scripture study into the daily patterns of your home?

THE CONNECTION

Set a goal to make scripture study more of a priority this month. Choose to incorporate one of the suggestions found in this chapter, or come up with ideas of your own. Another idea is to spend an evening asking each of your children to share his or her favorite scripture story about Jesus. Try to obtain a picture of the children's favorite stories to hang up in their bedrooms.

THE CELEBRATION

Hilary's Cheese Ball

1 package cream cheese
1 small jar Blue Rocha cheese
1 small jar Old English cheese
1 teaspoon Worcestershire sauce
2–3 green onions, chopped

Use a hand mixer to blend ingredients. Dip any variety of crackers into the cheese ball.

Hilary likes hers with pecans on top. If you like nuts, you will too!

THE LESSON FROM THE HOUSE OF JAIRUS

꙳ ꙳ ꙳

If you seek a household of scripture, embrace the stories of Jesus.

THE HOUSE OF PETER

A Household of

Holiness

THE FIFTH MONTH

Honor the Day That Is His

I t was an autumn afternoon in Capernaum. The holy Sabbath. After a day spent teaching and healing, Jesus and His disciples left the synagogue to spend the evening in Peter's home. Immediately after Jesus arrived, people in the house came to tell Him that Peter's mother-in-law was sick with a fever. "And he came and took her by the hand, and lifted her up" (Mark 1:31).

It was not long before the news had spread, and by the time the sun was setting, "all the city was gathered together at the door" (Mark 1:33). Alfred Edersheim explains, "To them, to all, had the door of hope now been opened. From all parts they bring them: mothers, widows, wives, fathers, children, husbands—their loved ones, the treasures they had almost lost; and the whole city throngs—a hushed, solemnised, over-awed multitude—expectant, waiting at the door of Simon's dwelling" (Edersheim, *Life and Times of Jesus*, 882). Once the Sabbath supper was over, Jesus left the home and walked the street, lifting the lowly and healing the sick.

The lesson taught in this home portrays a pattern of how our Sabbath days might be filled. The day began with church. Not simply attending church, but participating and playing an active role in the community. Within the synagogue Jesus taught, but He also had conversations with others who had come to worship—powerful conversations in which lives were changed and hearts were healed. After those sacred experiences, Jesus and His disciples arrived at a home where families were gathered. There was concern for a sick mother. Again, there was a powerful sense of community—people asking the Lord for His blessing, lifting the lowly, and strengthening one another's faith. Surely these families ate the Sabbath meal together, and once they were through, Jesus spent time visiting with mothers and fathers, children and loved ones, widows and the fatherless. He opened the door of hope and spent the evening lifting, healing, and blessing.

Take a few moments to consider how this Sabbath might compare to one of yours. The scriptures are clear on the description of the Sabbath. "Verily my sabbaths ye shall keep: for it is a sign between me and you throughout your generations; that ye may know that I am the Lord that doth sanctify you. Ye shall keep the sabbath therefore; for it is holy unto you . . . Wherefore the children of Israel shall keep the sabbath, to observe the sabbath . . . for a perpetual covenant" (Exodus 31:13–16). The Sabbath is set apart as a time for resting and refreshing.

In Ezekiel we read, "And hallow my sabbaths; and they shall be a sign between me and you, that ye may know that I am the Lord your God" (Ezekiel 20:20). To hallow means to keep holy, to sanctify, to respect, or to *make* holy.

In Mark, the Lord teaches, "The sabbath was made for man, and not man for the sabbath" (Mark 2:27). In other words, it is His gift to us.

As we consider these descriptions, we begin to see what the Lord intends for the Sabbath. We should *keep* the Sabbath day *holy.* Or in other words, we should set it apart

If requires observance, as in a keeping or a celebration. It should be hallowed, or made holy. It is a gift.

or consecrate it for the Lord. It requires *observance,* as in a keeping or a celebration. It should be *hallowed,* or made holy. It is a *gift.*

If the day is meant to be made holy, kept, set apart, celebrated, and valued as a gift, then we shouldn't wait until Sunday morning to prepare. Perhaps we should be preparing all week for the day the Lord set aside for rest and refreshing.

Maybe you could spend a little time reflecting on these questions:

What does the Sabbath mean to me?

_____

_____

_____

What purpose does the Sabbath achieve in my life?

_____
_____
_____

What purpose would I like the Sabbath to achieve?

_____
_____
_____

What are the distractions that are preventing that from happening right now?

_____
_____
_____

How could I focus my actions on achieving that purpose?

_____
_____
_____

The lesson we learn from Peter's house teaches some of the actions that can make our Sabbath more holy:
- Attend church.
- Be uplifted through worship.

- Add to the community of Saints we gather with.
- Spend time with family.
- Seek blessings from the Lord.
- Visit the sick, the weary, or the lonely.

Another form of worship that we practice in our family is to set aside one Sabbath every month for fasting. This sacred practice can help us become more sensitive to the Spirit and help us develop a more intimate relationship with Christ. It teaches us discipline and self-control and can make us more humble. The Bible records several instances when people observed a fast in order to receive a blessing from the Lord. We can fast for wisdom (see Acts 14:23), for protection (see Ezra 8:21–23), for help to gain victory (see Judges 20:26–28), to worship (see Luke 2:37), for healing (see Mark 9:25–29), or for strength (see Esther 4:16). Fasting on the Sabbath can help us make the day more holy. It requires sacrifice, but the sacrifice leads to a closer relationship with Christ. "If you don't feel strong desires for the manifestation of the glory of God, it is not because you have drunk deeply and are satisfied. It is because you have nibbled so long at the table of the world. Your soul is stuffed with small things, and there is no room for the great" (John Piper, *A Hunger for God: Desiring God through Fasting and Prayer* [Wheaton, Illinois: Crossway Books, 1997], 23). I am intrigued by the lesson found in the last line of this quote. I wonder how often our Sabbath is stuffed with small things, leaving no room for the great.

What are your thoughts on this idea?

_____

_____

_____

We recently sat down as a family to talk about how we want to honor the Lord's day. We began the conversation by talking about Christmas. It is one of our favorite holidays. We begin preparing for it months in advance. We talked about the food that we love to eat, the traditions we have, and the reasons why we look forward to the gathering. We made a list: new pajamas, ebelskivers for breakfast, fun games, and quiet moments gathered around burning candles when we remember the times we have seen the hand of the Lord in our lives. Those are just a few. It became clear that the reason we love Christmas isn't because it is December 25; it is because we have set apart that day as a celebration focused on Christ with good food, fun, and time spent talking about what is important. Then I asked if we might be able to set apart the Sabbath as a holy celebration similar to Christmas. If the day were filled with good food and fun and conversations centered on Christ, would it become a day we looked forward to, similar to the way we look forward to December 25? We decided to give it a try. We started establishing traditions that would intentionally set that day apart from every other day of the week. I call these our sweet Sabbath moments. In our home it is a family-only day. We spend time together playing games or making cookies. Grace loves to make and decorate sugar cookies; I like to make meringues. We trade off. For one hour each Sunday we gather in the family room with a journal and spend time cultivating what matters most. This is a time for goal setting

———————— ⸺ ⸺ ⸺ ————————

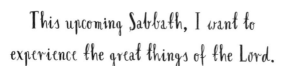

This upcoming Sabbath, I want to experience the great things of the Lord.

———————— ⸺ ⸺ ⸺ ————————

and family planning—a weekly time to center our life again, with God's purposes in mind. The evenings are for large family gathering. Married kids, aunts and uncles, cousins, and grandma and grandpa usually gather to eat dinner and share stories and laugh. With deliberately planning, Sundays have become my most favorite day of the week.

I wish we could gather together as mothers and talk about the ways we are intentionally setting apart the Sabbath in our homes. It would be so helpful to share ideas and traditions and recipes. These are the moments when I wish you all lived right next door.

But there is a way we could share and strengthen each other with our intentions to keep the Sabbath. What if we each posted our ideas on Instagram? We could use the hashtag #sweetsabbathmoments. It could become a place where we gather to share the ways we are making the Sabbath more intentional.

This upcoming Sabbath, I want to experience the great things of the Lord. I want my Sabbath to be a celebration, a time for refreshment, a gift. I long for it to become something I look forward to as I do a holiday—as a day set apart to spend time with family, rejoice in Christ, and rejuvenate my soul. So, this week I will do things differently. I will prepare. I can prepare my home so that there is order and choose a meal of simplicity with little work and cleanup required. I will prepare the clothing we will wear ahead of

All week I look forward to the one day when my life will settle, when I can breathe and refresh and rejuvenate. It is the day I still my soul. It is the day that is His.

time to make sure it is clean, pressed, and organized. I will prepare my heart by spending time in His word so that I am ready to be taught. I will listen to uplifting music. I will set apart moments of stillness.

Several months ago I found a quote that hangs on the side of my refrigerator. Lest your imagination carry you away, it is not one of those beautiful prints that you can find on Pinterest. It is scribbled in my write-this-down-fast-before-I-forget handwriting on a piece of white type paper, and there is a smudge of raspberry right at the bottom. I leave it on the fridge because it is a reminder of something I am trying to accomplish in my life—a prayer I carry in my heart all week long. "Lord, help me live an unhurried life" (Renee Swope). The Sabbath is my way of realizing that goal. All week I look forward to the one day when my life will settle, when I can breathe and refresh and rejuvenate. It is the day I still my soul. It is the day that is His.

Honor the Day That Is His

THE CONVERSATION

Mark 1:30–34

What are some things you notice about the Sabbath day as described in the first chapter of Mark? How often are those same practices part of your Sabbath day? Spend some time discussing how you might make your Sabbath worship more meaningful. Could you visit family? Maybe you could spend time with someone who is lonely or sick. Perhaps you will attend church with the intention to bless the lives of those you worship with.

THE CONNECTION

Plan ways for this upcoming Sabbath to be more meaningful. Write your ideas on a piece of paper, and hang the paper up where everyone in your family can refer to it throughout the day. Try to follow your plan. When the day is over, talk about the differences you noticed this Sabbath.

THE CELEBRATION

Apple Crisp

Mix and put into a glass baking dish:

>   4 cups sliced apples
>   ¼ cup water
>   1 teaspoon cinnamon
>   ½ teaspoon salt

Mix until crumbly and sprinkle over apples:

>   1 cup sugar
>   ¾ cup flour
>   ⅓ cup butter

Bake for 40 minutes at 350 degrees. Serve with vanilla ice cream.

The aroma of this apple crisp will fill your whole home. You might put it in the oven just as you begin your evening discussion and then dig in after you have finished setting your goals.

THE LESSON FROM THE HOUSE OF PETER

꙳ ꙳ ꙳

If you seek a household of holiness, honor the day that is His.

THE HOUSE IN JERUSALEM

A Household of

Unity

Do Nice. Be Sweet.

I t was the man's best room. The upper chamber, a large room made ready for the Paschal supper. He had provided all that was needed for the supper—the wine for the cups, the cakes of unleavened bread, and the bitter herbs. The festive lamps were lit. Just as the sun was beginning to set, Jesus and His disciples walked down from the Mount of Olives and into the Holy City, which was adorned in jubilant attire. The streets were filled with worshippers, the hills dotted with the bright flowers of early spring, the temple lit up by the slanting rays of the setting sun. Leaving the splendid view behind them, Jesus and His Apostles would have entered the upper chamber, festively lit and prepared for the gathering.

It was a gathering in which the disciples would be taught by the Master. The subjects would include loyalty, sacrifice, and service. The washing of feet, the partaking of bread and wine, the exit of one whose heart was intent on betrayal—all of these memories must have been seared into the hearts of the disciples. Surely they must have reflected back on this night during the days that followed. Perhaps they remembered the specifics of the conversation, and in particular the teaching from the Master. In truth, several chapters could be devoted to the teaching that took place around that table in the upper chamber on that sacred evening, but one simple lesson stands out to me every time.

It comes from a conversation that took place between Peter and Jesus at the end of the meal. There was a pause as Jesus prepared Peter for what was about to take place. The lesson contained a warning, a promise, and an admonition. The warning was that Satan wanted Peter's soul. The promise was that the Lord Himself had prayed for Peter, that his faith would not fail. The admonition was one that Peter would fulfill every day following for the remainder of his life—strengthen your brothers (see Luke 22:31–32).

We live in a world fraught with spiritual peril. Our beliefs are being tested on every side. Daily we have moments in which we must choose whether we will stand true to our beliefs or deny the faith.

This warning, promise, and admonition could benefit each of our homes. It is true that Satan is intent on destroying each of us; it is true also that the greatest desire of the

Lord is that our faith will not fail. We live in a world fraught with spiritual peril. Our beliefs are being tested on every side. Daily we have moments in which we must choose whether we will stand true to our beliefs or deny the faith. The Savior knows this about the world we live in. It is what makes His counsel to Peter so interesting. His advice was not for Peter to simply look out for himself; rather, it was to strengthen his brethren. Once Peter had "turned again," or become converted, the Lord wanted him to strengthen his brothers.

This gathering and strengthening is prominent in the Lord's teaching. Throughout the scriptures, we find verses admonishing us to gather for church, for prayer, and even for meals. The doctrine of unity is an essential teaching in the New Testament: "And they, continuing daily with one accord in the temple, and breaking bread from house to house, did eat their meat with gladness and singleness of heart, praising God, and having favour with all the people" (Acts 2:46–47). In the book of Acts we read of a time when many were gathered together praying (see Acts 12:12). In Thessalonians we read of a group who gathered together so they would not be shaken in mind or troubled (see 2 Thessalonians 2:1–2). In Esther we read of a time when all of the Lord's people were gathered together to fast in behalf of a cause that had the power to save them (see Esther 4:1–17). These are just a few examples of gathering that fill the pages of scripture.

From the house with the upper chamber we learn the importance of gathering and strengthening. Consider your own home for a minute. When do you gather? Perhaps you gather for meals, family prayer, or in the evening to discuss sacred topics, play games, or counsel together. Moments of gathering could include working in the yard or completing a project in the house. These gatherings could include traditions that take place around holidays or other occasions.

Create a list of the times when your family gathers:

_____

_____

_____

In our family we love to gather, and we have created events specifically for that purpose. My mother taught me an important lesson in this regard. When we were younger, there were certain nights set aside for family. These nights were sacred to our family, and we were rarely allowed to miss the gatherings. However, as we grew older and married and had families of our own, these original family nights together were extended as an invitation—we were always invited, but the needs of our individual families came first.

I have tried to implement this in my own family. When my children were young, we had one night set aside for our family. We played games, went out for ice cream, completed projects in the yard or home, or learned from the scriptures about topics our family needed to focus on at that time. Those nights, set apart for gathering, strengthened our family relationships.

Now my kids are older. Most of them are in college. But

we still extend invitations for them to gather at home. My kids know that on Monday nights in the summer I walk to the shave ice shack down the street from our home. Often they will text me to find out what time I am going and drive home to join me.

The same is true for my own mother. Every Sunday night she makes dinner for the family. Every single Sunday night. It is her invitation to gather. I have six siblings, and between us there are thirty grandchildren, and we are blessed to all live very near one another. Everyone is invited to these Sunday dinners. We attend as we can. Sometimes only two or three families show up, but our favorite is when the schedules work out just right for all forty-five of us to gather on Sunday night for dinner. Let me be honest—it is a circus. But I love the experiences and memories that come as we gather there. It is a sacrifice on my mom's part, but it is worth it to her. She loves the times of gathering.

One of the greatest blessings that can come from gathering is the strengthening that takes place. This strengthening is crucial for family unity. Family relationships are hard. I don't know about your home, but in our home, sibling rivalry was a daily occurrence. I am reminded of two letters written to God by young children. The first said, "Dear God, I bet it is very hard for you to love all of everybody in the whole world. There are only four people in our family and I can never do it."

The second: "Maybe Cain and Abel would not kill each other so much if they had their own rooms. It works with my brother." Lest you think that just gathering your family together will solve all of the problems, let me be clear: there is a great deal of strengthening that must take place first in order to create the unity we seek to achieve. Gathering is the fun part. Strengthening requires work.

I recently stumbled across an old southern phrase that I want to hang permanently on the walls of my kitchen. The phrase is simple: "Do nice. Be sweet." In a very simple way, strengthening requires mastering those two ideals.

I grew up with a mother who believed in nice. Above all else, choosing the nice thing to do ruled the day. I would come home from school fed up with my friends and complaining about how ruthless ninth-grade girls could be, and my mother would say four words: "Be nice. Beeee nice." Emphasis on the *be* the second time. Try it. Yep. That's just how it would sound. The teacher who had given an unfair

Do nice. Be sweet.

grade, the boy who had been rude, the mother down the street who assumed something that wasn't right about a situation—all received the same consideration. Be nice, *be* nice. It wasn't just a phrase my mom carried in her back pocket; it was a sentiment she wore like a mantle. My mom always chose nice first. She taught us to look for the best in someone, to find the root of the problem behind the unkind behavior, to offer understanding first—always. I am who I am because of her example. Sometimes it is easier to be nice to our friends and less easy to be nice to our family. Learning niceness is one of the things we work on the most in our home. Here are two phrases that have helped as we have tried to work on being nice within the walls of our home: *assume the best* and *I love you because.*

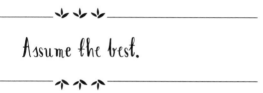

Assume the best.

Assume the best is a phrase I learned from a good friend with whom I was studying the Old Testament. Some of the stories in the Bible are filled with disturbing situations. We can't help but wonder about some of the choices and actions that are made. Often we read one or two verses and question what is taking place.

One afternoon, my friend and I were discussing some of the stories that leave you asking questions, and my friend said something I have never forgotten: "When it comes to a part of the Bible that I don't understand, I always tell myself to assume the best." I tried it, and it worked! So then I started applying that advice to situations in my own life. When someone forgot to send an invitation to an event that everyone else went to, when a friend walked right past me in church without saying a word, or when someone didn't follow through on an assignment and left me hanging, I did what my friend had suggested—I assumed the best.

Interestingly, in most situations, assuming the best was

exactly the right thing to do. I found that there was generally a reason that made complete sense behind a behavior that hadn't made any sense at all. It works particularly well when I try to apply it with my children and my siblings. Assuming the best has allowed me to become more forgiving of the faults I would normally find in others. It has helped me learn to be nice.

"I love you because" is a phrase that helps us look more deeply into what it is we love most about the people closest to us.

I love you because is a phrase that helps us look more deeply into what it is we love most about the people closest to us. It teaches us to pay attention to the characteristics and qualities we admire. Instead of quickly saying "I love you" in a passing moment, adding a "because" requires us to stop and focus more carefully on the person we are speaking with. The added reflection strengthens the relationship and uplifts the heart. Often, describing the "because" is one of nicest things we can say to someone.

Assuming the best and taking the time to express why we love each member of our family can help strengthen the unity in our home. But these two concepts alone are not enough. Another key element in strengthening has to do with sweetness.

There is a fruit vendor who visits our neighborhood on a regular basis. He comes to the door with his apron pockets filled with fruit. He doesn't tell you what he has to offer in the back of his truck; he shows you. Pulling an apple out of one pocket, he slices it and offers you a piece, leaving the rest of the apple to rest on the windowsill. Next, a slice of orange. Last, a slice of grapefruit. It doesn't take long to notice when this fruit man has been to the neighborhood. All you have to do is walk down the street to see the evidence of his visit. Fruit fills the windowsills of every home. The fruit man is known for his fruit. It is fresh, but most of all, it is sweet. Sweeter than anything you could buy in the produce section of a grocery store.

Sometimes when I read about the fruits of the Spirit found in Galatians, I think about the fruit man who visits my home. These are fruits that cannot be experienced just by talking about them—they must be shown. Think for a minute about these fruits: love, joy, peace, patience, kindness, goodness, faithfulness, gentleness, and self-control (see Galatians 5:22–23). If our homes are filled with these attributes, these fruits of the Spirit, there will be a sweetness that will strengthen all who live within.

"Now thanks be unto God, which always causeth us to triumph in Christ, . . . for we are unto God a sweet savour of Christ" (2 Corinthians 2:14–15). Part of creating a Christ-centered home is discovering a way to allow the sweet savor of Christ to permeate our hearts and allow that spirit to fill our homes with actions that bear witness of the fruit.

Fruits of the Spirit
Love
Joy
Peace
Patience
Kindness
Goodness
Faithfulness
Gentleness
Self-Control

What are some ways that these attributes are made manifest in your home?

_____

_____

_____

What could you do to help teach these attributes so that all family members might experience an increase of the fruits of the Spirit in their lives?

_____

_____

_____

Teaching the attributes of the Spirit requires a conscious effort. I remember vividly a summer afternoon when my two boys were playing in the basement together. I heard an argument beginning. It was my nature to end an argument right as it started, before things escalated, so I immediately called Caleb to the bottom of the stairs. At three years old, he was the oldest and the easiest to reason with. "Caleb," I said, in a voice filled with admonition, "please choose the right." It was a catchphrase we used often in our home, short for making the right choice no matter what situation you were in. His reply was immediate: "I am, Mom, but Josh is on the left." Do you know those moments when it is important to keep a straight face as a mother, but your insides are filled with a gigantic chuckle? This was one of those. Raising two boys less than eighteen months apart required me to be constantly teaching in order for the fruits of the Spirit to find a place in our home. We worked on creating love and peace and kindness daily. My college-age kids still talk about what happened in our home when there was an argument between two siblings. They would have to sit cross-legged facing each other and stay there until they could each say three nice things about the other. The kindness couldn't be rushed or casual; the response had to be genuine. Once they had each said the three kind things they loved about the other, they hugged and then the day continued on. It was a simple way of bringing the Spirit back into our home after a moment of contention, and it worked every time.

A home based on unity would be filled with the pure love of Christ. It would include working together, fun, kindness, open dialogue, gathering together, learning to resolve differences, loyalty, trust, and respect. There would be moments of gathering and moments of strengthening filled with an abundance of sweetness, the sweet savor of Christ.

Do Nice. Be Sweet.

THE CONVERSATION

LUKE 22:31-32

What do you think it means to strengthen someone? Can you think of particular ways that Peter strengthened the other disciples throughout his life? How could the attributes of being nice and sweet add to the strength of your family?

THE CONNECTION

Get one piece of paper for each member of your family. Write the name of one family member on the top of each piece. Underneath the person's name, write the phrase "I love you because . . ." Hang the papers in a room your family walks through on a regular basis. All month long, have family members take the time to fill up those papers as they notice things they love about each family member. At the end of the month, make sure each person puts his or her paper in a safe place where they can read it often.

THE CELEBRATION

Coconut Lime Popcorn

Pop a large bowl of popcorn.

Melt ½ cup of coconut oil and pour over the popcorn.

Sprinkle with sea salt.

Add a splash of lime juice and stir.

THE LESSON FROM
THE HOUSE IN JERUSALEM

⚜ ⚜ ⚜

*If you seek a household of unity,
do nice and be sweet.*

THE HOUSE
IN CAPERNAUM

A Household of

Grace

Find Grace in the Ordinary

The Savior was in Capernaum. While there, a tax collector approached Peter and asked if his master would be paying the tribute, or, in other words, the temple tax. Peter answered yes and then walked into the home where Jesus was. Jesus asked Peter, "What thinkest thou, Simon? of whom do the kings of the earth take custom or tribute? of their own children, or of strangers?" Peter answered, "Of strangers." So Jesus replied, "Then are the children free" (Matthew 17:25–26).

It must have become instantly clear to Peter in that moment that the temple is God's house, and therefore the Son of God would be exempt from the temple tax. Since an earthly prince would obviously not pay a tax on his own home, of course Jesus should not be expected to pay taxes on the temple.

But the lesson was not over. Jesus understood the particulars of the financial situation the apostles faced at the time; they barely had the means to get by. But He also knew the condition of the hearts of those who came collecting. With those two things in mind, He answered Peter,

"Notwithstanding, lest we should offend them, go thou to the sea, and cast an hook, and take up the fish that first cometh up; and when thou hast opened his mouth, thou shalt find a piece of money: that take, and give unto them for me and thee" (Matthew 17:27).

Consider the miracle found in this ordinary story. At face value, we see a simple conversation about paying taxes and a man who goes fishing at a lake. In reality, however, the story contains so much more. The miracle is found in the ordinary—that Jesus knew there was a fish in the lake with a coin in its mouth, that the coin would be the right amount for the taxes, that Peter would throw the line into the right place in the lake, that the right fish would be the first to take

Instances of orchestrated grace are regular occurrences that make up the ordinary details of our lives. Somehow we need to learn to open up our eyes and recognize them when they happen. You have experienced moments like these. We all have.

the hook. It is all of these ordinary details carefully orchestrated together that brought to pass the miracle. Through these details Peter experienced grace, an enabling power beyond his own that allowed Christ's purposes to be fulfilled.

What is most fascinating to me about this story is that experiences like this don't happen only in Matthew chapter 14; they take place on a regular basis, all of the time. Instances of orchestrated grace are regular occurrences that make up the ordinary details of our lives. Somehow we need

Grace: the times when the ordinary details of life are orchestrated in such a way that you are reminded heaven has not forgotten you.

to learn to open up our eyes and recognize them when they happen. You have experienced moments like these. We all have. They are found in the sunset just after your mother's funeral, the words of a song that comes on the radio as you are driving away from a discouraging doctor's visit, the unexpected text from a friend. These are the times when the ordinary details of life are orchestrated in such a way that you are reminded heaven has not forgotten you.

I love these orchestrated moments, the times when we experience the tender mercies of the Lord and are instantly reminded of His loving kindness. There was one morning I was preparing to speak at a huge event. I was backstage going over my notes, just waiting for the event to start. Everything was in order except for the black satin bow that I was using as a belt. It would not stay tied. Every three minutes I would look down and see that it had come undone again. It was going to be a problem on stage. I went into the women's restroom to see if I could find a solution. Standing in front of the mirror, I retied the bow several times to see if I could get it tight enough to stay. It didn't matter how many times I tried—after a few minutes the loops would slip right out. After several attempts, the woman who runs the event came into the bathroom. She walked into the second stall. "How is it going?" she asked as she shut the door and locked the stall.

"Terrible," I replied. "I can't get this bow to stay tied. You wouldn't happen to have a safety pin?" She immediately started laughing. That was awkward. I wasn't sure what was so funny about me asking for a safety pin. My mind was filled with foreboding about the potential disaster that was going to take place on stage. She told me to hand my phone over the stall. I couldn't figure out what was going on, but I obliged—she was my boss, after all. I heard her take a picture, and then she handed my phone back out to me. I looked to see what had been so humorous, and there,

He had remembered me in my
simple time of need.

carefully clasped onto the handle of the inside of the bathroom stall, was a safety pin. Exactly what I most needed in the moment I needed it. Orchestrated. I was reminded once again that often what we think of as a coincidence is really a tender mercy from the Lord. He had remembered me in my simple time of need.

The word *remembered* is one of my favorite words to look for when I read the Bible. I keep a list of the moments when God remembers His people. We read in Genesis 8:1 that God remembered Noah after the flood, in Genesis 30:22 that "God remembered Rachel, and God hearkened unto her, and opened her womb," and in Genesis 19:29, we are told that God remembered Abraham. I love the verse in Exodus, just before the Lord delivered the children of Israel, that says, "God remembered his covenant with Abraham, with Isaac, and with Jacob. And God looked upon the children of Israel, and God had respect unto them" (Exodus 2:24–25). Perhaps my very favorite is from the book of Samuel, when Hannah approached the Lord in an abundance of grief and begged, "Remember me" (1 Samuel 1:11). A few verses later, we see one small phrase that changed Hannah's life: "And the Lord remembered her" (1 Samuel 1:19). Every time I read that verse, I think to myself, *if the Lord remembered Hannah in her moment of need, then He will remember me.* I love what Angie Smith teaches about the word *remember*: "When we see scripture use the phrase, 'God remembered,' it doesn't mean He forgets. It means, 'He acts'" (Angie Smith, *Seamless: Understanding the Bible as One Complete Story* [Nashville, Tennessee: LifeWay Press, 2015], 66).

It is important to teach our families to recognize when the Lord keeps His promises. Learning to be aware of the times when God remembers us requires watching for those carefully orchestrated details in the midst of our ordinary days. It is not a practice that comes easily. Think of the children of Israel, who allowed the miracle from heaven, the daily manna, to become commonplace and ordinary. I love learning from others who have made the practice of remembering God's grace part of the pattern of their lives.

Can you think of a time when the Lord remembered you or someone in your family?

_____

_____

_____

Ann Voskamp is a woman I look up to and admire. Several years ago she decided to write down and keep track of God's gifts in her life so that she might more fully recognize His ordinary, amazing grace. By June 11, 2012, she was on reason number 3,651. She doesn't just write down the big things; she finds grace in the small things—3,652, long grass early in the morning; 3,653, laughing with Jessica and Annie; 3,656, full, soapy cleaning buckets and dirty floors. Her journey reminds me of some song lyrics that describe this practice of remembering: "You're rich in love and You're slow to anger, Your name is great and Your heart is kind, for all Your goodness I will keep on singing, ten thousand reasons for my heart to find" (Matt Redman, "10,000 Reasons [Bless the Lord]," 2011). I want to teach my children to watch for His goodness, to keep track of their own 10,000 reasons, to discover His ordinary, amazing grace every single day.

My oldest son, Caleb, lived in Serbia and Croatia for two years. We would write each other every Monday. On one occasion he told me he had started keeping a Book of Evidences—a journal of the times when he experienced the hand of the Lord in his life. After talking to him, I went to a bookstore and purchased several inexpensive journals. I had the store imprint "Book of Evidences" on each cover. I challenged my family to start keeping a record of our dealings with the Lord just like Caleb was doing—a record of prayers answered, times when they felt promptings from the Spirit, and experiences when they witnessed the hand of the Lord in their lives. It was a way to help us record the times when we were remembered by Him. "Remember . . . I have formed thee. . . . thou shalt not be forgotten of me" (Isaiah 44:21).

I had an epiphany shortly after I started keeping my book of evidences. I was reading the scriptures, and I started flipping through the pages. I saw the names written at the top of the pages—Joshua, Esther, Job, Matthew, Peter—and I realized that the pages of scripture had become, in a sense, each person's Book of Evidences. These were records of their dealings with the Lord. A record of prayers answered, times when they felt promptings, and experiences in which they had witnessed the hand of the Lord in their lives. The scriptures were a record and a witness that the Lord had remembered them—the same way He remembers us.

Perhaps there is a purpose for keeping a record of that truth.

Maybe it is so we will remember Him.

Find Grace in the Ordinary

THE CONVERSATION

Matthew 17:25–27

Read the story about the temple tax and Peter's fishing trip. What is it about those ordinary details being orchestrated by God that makes it so miraculous? What does this story teach us about grace?

THE CONNECTION

Get a journal or notebook for every member of your family. Write or imprint the words "Book of Evidences" on the cover or inside front page. Invite your family members to keep track of the moments during the day when they are remembered by the Lord. Record these tender mercies all month long. At the end of the month, spend an evening sharing these moments together as a family.

THE CELEBRATION

Aunt Mickie's Hot Fudge Sauce

1 can sweetened condensed milk
2 tablespoons butter
1 square unsweetened chocolate
1 teaspoon vanilla

Heat butter and condensed milk on medium low heat until warm. Add the chocolate and stir until smooth. Then add vanilla. If it is too thick, add a little bit of water.

Serve over ice cream.

Using coconut oil instead of butter gives this chocolate syrup a rich and distinct flavor. It is especially delicious over mint chocolate chip or cookie dough ice cream.

THE LESSON FROM
THE HOUSE IN CAPERNAUM

⋆ ⋆ ⋆

If you seek a household of grace, discover it in the ordinary.

THE HOUSE IN CANA

A Household of

Change

Forget Your Perfect Offering

I t was the marriage in Cana of Galilee. I like to imagine it taking place in a house in a little town with village gardens and orchards nearby. The house would have been festively adorned with lamps and candlesticks, and the guests would have been enjoying a celebratory evening meal.

It was sometime during the evening when Mary turned to Jesus and said, "They have no wine" (John 2:3). Many have questioned Mary's motives in posing this statement. Perhaps it was simply due to her absolute confidence in Jesus. She knew that He would know exactly what to do. With this confidence, she asked the servants to do exactly as Jesus asked. So six waterpots of stone were filled with water to the brim, and then the servants drew from them and took the contents to the governor of the feast, who declared it as good wine.

This, the first of Jesus' miracles, was more than just turning water into wine. It was symbolic of the miracles that would follow—a witness of the power Jesus Christ has to change whatever He touches. Water to wine. Making blind to see. The unclean to clean again. The sick, whole. At the

root of every miracle Jesus performed there was change—
and this truth was made manifest in one of the very first
miracles He performed. My favorite line of this whole story
is found at the end of verse eleven: "His disciples believed
on Him" (John 2:11).

This, the first of Jesus' miracles, was more than just turning water into wine. It was symbolic of the miracles that would follow—a witness of the power Jesus Christ has to change whatever He touches.

As true followers of Jesus Christ, we too must come to
believe in the absolute power Christ has to change. He holds
the power to change hearts, to change lives, to change cir-
cumstance. Great comfort accompanies this powerful truth,
for when we fully grasp the reality of that knowledge, we
realize that there is no earthly care that cannot be overcome
through Him. Not one of us is perfect. Each of us has something that needs to be changed. And yet, we hold onto that
thing, often not knowing how to let it go, leave it behind, or
change it for the better. We forget that He has the power to
overcome it if we will just let Him.

I love the wisdom in this line by Leonard Cohen:
"Forget your perfect offering—there's a crack in everything—that's how the light gets in" ("Anthem," Columbia

Forget your perfect offering—there's a crack in everything—that's how the light gets in.

—Leonard Cohen

Records, 1992). Instead of focusing on the perfection we think we have to offer, maybe we need to look harder at the cracks in us, for it is within the cracks that we will discover His light and therefore discover Him. It is there, within the cracks, that He will be working, if we allow Him to. The Lord knows who we are, but even more importantly, He knows who we are meant to become. The miracle takes place when we allow Him to make the changes that are necessary for us to turn "the water of our felt want into the wine of His giving" (Edersheim, *Life and Times of Jesus*, 729). Sometimes that change can only take place when we come to remember who we are in His eyes. If we get lost in the person the world thinks we are, we may never become the person the Lord knows that we can be.

How have you discovered the light of the Lord within the cracks that make up your offering?

_____

_____

_____

I love the story of the man from the Gadarenes. This is a man who "had devils long time, and ware no clothes, neither abode in any house" (Luke 8:27). When the man saw Jesus, he cried out and fell down at His feet. I love the first words Jesus says to him. He looked past the outward appearance, past the lack of clothes, the homelessness, the affliction that had taken over his life, and asked, "What is thy name?" (Luke 8:30). Before the miracle could take place, Jesus had to remind the man who he really was. After the miracle had taken place, Jesus gave the man counsel meant to help him hold on to the change that had taken place in his life: "Return to thine own house, and shew how great things God hath done unto thee" (Luke 8:39). Go home. There is strength there. Talk to the people in your home about God and the great things He has done for you.

Oh, there is so much that I love about this story. I think about my own children. It is so important that we take the time to remind them of who they are in the Lord's eyes and who they have the potential to become. **What are some ways you could be better at doing this?**

_____

_____

_____

In times of distress, when things are not as they should be with our children, we need to remember to look past the affliction that has taken over their lives and help to remind them who they really are underneath all the weight they carry and the disguise that hides the truth. **How could you learn to look deeper than the affliction and see the good?**

_____

_____

_____

Last, we must remember to talk in our homes about the great things of God and the power He has to help us change. Can you remember a time when you experienced a much-needed change through the help of the Lord?

_____

_____

_____

Sometimes we get so caught up in our "perfect offering" that we forget to seek for the light seeping through the cracks. We forget to let the Lord do His work. We forget the power He has to change whatever He touches.

Part of the work we do within the walls of our homes is to help our children remember who they are. The world will try to get in the way of this. Sometimes friends will cause a distraction. Voices of doubt will whisper damaging words in

Sometimes we get so caught up in our "perfect offering" that we forget to seek for the light seeping through the cracks. We forget to let the Lord do His work.

quiet moments. Somehow we need to find ways to reaffirm the great things the Lord sees in each of them.

As our children were born, we gave each one of them two names. One from the Bible, and one from our family, so that they could be true to the names they bore and live up to the potential of those who had gone before. After the first few years of each child's life, in the stage of independence that accompanies the toddler phase, I also gave each of my children a word that encompassed one of his or her greatest qualities. Caleb's word is *wisdom*, Josh's is *strength*, Garett's is *valor*, Meg's is *joy*, and Grace's is *miracle*. For many years I wore these words on a necklace to remind me of our children's gifts. Recently my husband, Greg, and I gathered together five huge tree stumps to place around our fire pit. Late one afternoon and into the evening I etched those words into the fresh wood of each trunk. I wanted my children to have a visual reminder of the gift I saw in them, the gift God had given them, and to help them live up to the potential that gift will help them realize. I have come to believe that constant reminders of the good we see in our children will become a great strength to them as they face a troubled world.

Many years ago, I was driving with a friend along the back roads of North Carolina. Our conversation was filled with family, life pursuits, and the burden of trying to balance everything. At one point my friend turned to me and said, "I think I know what your gifting is, do you?" I was immediately intrigued by the thought of this "gifting," a gift that came from God, and what she thought it might be. "It's the gift of insight," she responded after a short silence.

"That is your gifting." The conversation changed course after that. We arrived at our destination. Now it has been years since that moment took place. Perhaps my friend would not even remember it happened. But I have thought back on those few minutes time and time again. That conversation has carried me through moments of fear, it has strengthened me in moments of discouragement and doubt, and in times of failure I have whispered her words over and over in my mind. *I have the gift of insight. It is one thing I am good at. If no one else believes it about me, that's okay. My friend Jennie does.*

What is your gift? Can you think of a word that might represent a gift of each of your family members?

_____

_____

_____

I believe there is a great power that comes when we set aside the illusion of a perfect offering.

I believe there is a great power that comes when we turn again to Christ and allow Him to fill our cracks with light.

I believe there is a great power that comes when we grasp hold of the miraculous reality that Jesus Christ has the power to change everything He touches.

I believe there is a great power that comes from knowing who we are.

I believe there is a great power that comes from recognizing His gifts within us.

Forget Your Perfect Offering

THE CONVERSATION

John 2:1-11 and Luke 8:27-39

What could you do to help your children remember who they are and to fully grasp the hope of what they could become by turning their lives over to the Lord? How could you help your children recognize their gifts? Is your home a place where a perfect offering is expected, or do you allow room and acceptance for people to experience change? Do you speak of the great things of God in your home? In times of distress, when someone in your family has taken a wrong turn, do you lead them to Jesus Christ and remind them of the power He has to change?

THE CONNECTION

Spend one evening coming up with a word to describe each member of your family. Consider the gifts each person has been given from God. Focus on what makes each one unique and special. Help your family members see the good that God sees in them.

THE CELEBRATION

Lime Sherbet Floats

Place two scoops of lime sherbet into a cup.

Fill the cup with lemon-lime soda.

This dessert is similar to root beer floats, but the fruit sherbet adds a lighter flavor. Any flavor of sherbet will work. It's a fun new twist to an old favorite.

THE LESSON FROM
THE HOUSE IN CANA

⋎ ⋎ ⋎

If you seek a household of change,
forget your perfect offering.

THE HOUSE THAT WAS FULL

A Household of

Love

A Refuge for Weary Travelers

Several months ago I was reading a blog post by a favorite author and friend of mine. We share many of the same passions; we also share the same name. There was a line in her post that left me pondering for many weeks afterward. It was simple, yet profound: "People don't need a fixer, they need a journeyer" (Emily P. Freeman, http://www

> People don't need a fixer,
> they need a journeyer.

—Emily P. Freeman

.incourage.me/2015/07/what-to-do-when-you-dont-have -an-answer.html). I have learned through experience that this is true. So often we want to help by fixing, finding the solution, or solving the problem. Sometimes we do not have the knowledge or capacity to resolve the problem. What if, in those times, we became a fellow journeyer and accompanied the person with the heavy load to the One who can fix all things?

Many people had gathered to the home where Jesus taught—so many that there was no more room in the house. Even the doorway and porch were completely full. Having heard that the Savior was teaching there, a group of men brought their friend who lay sick with palsy. It didn't take long before the four men realized they were not going to be able to get inside the home. But they didn't give up. The scriptures tell us, "They sought means to bring him in, and to lay him before [the Lord]" (Luke 5:18).

These friends came up with a plan. "They went upon the housetop, and let him down through the tiling with his couch into the midst before Jesus" (Luke 5:19). Now, stop and consider this for a minute. How did the four men get that man *and* his couch onto the roof and then down into the room where Jesus was? It couldn't have been easy. Who would hold the man on the couch? We must also keep in mind that the roof was not the final destination. Once they got on the roof, there was more work to be done. In Mark 2 we learn that the roof had to be uncovered and broken up. That must have required a lot of effort. Then the four men had to lower the couch carefully to where Jesus was. When I think of the part these four friends played in this process, I think of someone there to lift, another to support, one to hold on to, and another to add strength where it was needed.

Once they had lowered the man carefully into the room where Jesus was, a very interesting conversation took place. Both accounts in the New Testament phrase this conversation exactly the same way. We read, "When Jesus saw *their* faith, he said unto the sick of the palsy, Son, thy sins be forgiven thee" (Mark 2:5; emphasis added). Take note of the word *their*. Whose faith is the Savior talking about? The line doesn't read, "When Jesus saw *his* faith," it reads, "When Jesus saw *their* faith." Is He talking about the four friends? The ones who lifted, supported, held on to, and strengthened their friend? Was it through both the great lengths of their effort and the great faith of these friends that the Lord was able to heal this man? Is the same true today? Sometimes when I read this chapter I stop and ask myself, *to what lengths would I go to bring a friend to Christ?*

What are your thoughts?

_____

_____

_____

There is much we can learn from this story. First, we must consider the true intent of the four men. They, in and of themselves, could not heal this man. They could not fix the ailment. They could not tell the man what to believe or how to live his life. Their responsibility was simple and yet profound—their only responsibility was to bring their friend to Jesus. They were not the healers or the teachers, but they could bring their friend to the One who could heal, to the One who could teach. They became journeyers, not fixers. Their journey required faith. It also required lifting, supporting, strengthening, and holding on.

Sometimes I think we get confused. We become so intent on fixing the problem ourselves that we don't allow the Savior to do what He is best at—saving. The lesson from this home is clear—we have a responsibility as Christians to

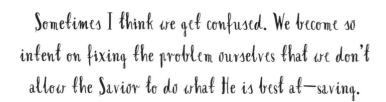

Sometimes I think we get confused. We become so intent on fixing the problem ourselves that we don't allow the Savior to do what He is best at—saving.

bring others to Jesus Christ through our service. This service might include lifting a heart, helping to support someone's burden, strengthening commitment, or encouraging others to hold on to their faith. It is often the times when we minister as Jesus would if He were here that prompt others to develop or strengthen their own relationship with the Lord.

I will never forget a time when my heart was filled to bursting with heavy thoughts. My sister's family was carrying a heavy emotional burden that they didn't have strength to bear. We had gathered as a family to offer support, but we couldn't fix the situation for them, and that was heartbreaking. Another family member, my sister-in-law, had called the day before to say that her husband had lost his job and that they were certain to lose their home. She didn't know what to do. Oh, how I longed to be able to come up with a solution that would fix that problem, but I couldn't. I also had a dear friend who was struggling with a problem that had the potential to destroy her life and her family. We had prayed and fasted together, and yet I knew deep within my heart I did not have the knowledge required to fix the challenge she was facing. I was discouraged, and I prayed for heaven's help to know what I might do.

Immediately an impression settled into my heart. My responsibility was not to fix the burdens these families were carrying; my responsibility was to journey with them and to help bring them closer to Christ. I could not save them, but He could. I knew the Savior would know what to do. He would know how to help heal their hearts; He could lead them in the direction they needed to go. His purpose would not fail, and His hand would not be stayed. Through His great wisdom and His marvelous ways, He would do what was right in their lives. I could lift, support, strengthen, and hold on, and I could add my faith. The Savior would do the rest.

Often the greatest thing we can do for others is to lead them closer to the Lord. We can do that by sharing what we know of Him from the feelings within our hearts. Perhaps, through us, others will come to understand what He teaches, to feel how He loves, and they will come to know His heart because they have come to know ours.

It is important that we learn to love and that we teach our families this attribute of Jesus. It is the tradition in our family, and has been for many generations, to invite those who are struggling into our hearts and our homes. My mother learned from her mother that we don't turn friends away. It doesn't matter what church they attend, what color their skin is, or what life problems they struggle with. All are welcome. In our home we try not to judge where a person has come from or where they are now. All that matters is where they are going and the companions they will have to travel with. We don't want anyone to travel alone. We offer our friendship, but more importantly, we talk of Jesus. There is no companion greater to travel with than the Lord Himself. Usually these conversations take place because we have invited someone into our home for an afternoon or for dinner. Sometimes we invite the person on a road trip. We try to reach out in the hallways at school, or during a sporting practice, or at an event. But sometimes the Lord has required more from us.

There is one autumn season I will never forget. It was the autumn that began with a prompting. My girls and I were traveling in the car together just before school started, and I said, "I want our home to be the type of home where people would feel something good. I want people to come to our doorstep and find a welcoming home where they feel safe. I wish it would be a home where people came to talk about Jesus." Then I asked my girls if we could try for the whole school year to have a home like that.

In October, a boy from the lacrosse team my husband coached showed up at the door with tears streaming down his face. He and my husband had talked several times over the summer about some struggles he was going through. Now he was finally ready to turn his life around. He didn't feel he could do it in his current situation. He asked if there was any way he could come live with us for a time so he could go to church with us and read the scriptures with us and let the Lord change his life. That night we cleaned out a room upstairs, and Ian moved in. About two weeks later, my sister-in-law and her daughter showed up at our door. Their life had taken an unexpected turn and they needed a place to stay. We moved the girls out of their bedroom and put my sister-in-law and her daughter there. Then we put up bunk beds next to the piano in the living room and created two makeshift closets for my girls to put their clothes in. Then two of our sons returned home unexpectedly and needed a place to stay for several months, so we put one under the ping pong table in the basement and the other bunked up in the room with Ian. Our house was full to bursting.

There was a moment when I questioned our capacity. I knelt in prayer before the Lord to let Him know we didn't have enough room or enough money for what had shown up on the doorstep. I will never forget the prompting that came through the Spirit on that afternoon: *Is the space for the ping pong table more important than the boy in the bedroom upstairs? Is the music room more important than the family whose life has been turned upside down? You provide the space,* the Spirit whispered, *God will provide the means.*

I have never forgotten that lesson. Every time I walk past my ping pong table I am reminded that God's work is not about objects; rather, it is about people. What I remember from those months when nine of us lived under one roof is not the mountain of laundry, the constant clutter, or the grocery bill. It is the nights we spent around the kitchen table eating together and then gathering to the family room. We piled onto the couches, squished tight and snuggled together, Ian took his favorite spot in front of the fireplace and we laughed, we strengthened each other, and we talked of Christ—of His forgiveness, His enabling grace, and the power of His love.

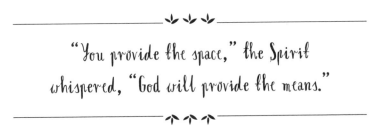

"You provide the space," the Spirit whispered, "God will provide the means."

Our house became a refuge for weary travelers. A place of safety. A place where people gathered to talk about Jesus. My house had become exactly what I had wished it might for that school year. Not in the way I had envisioned, but in the way God had envisioned.

What does God have in mind for your home this year? Could you set a goal as a family to open your hearts and be willing to bring a friend to Christ? The friend doesn't need to move into your home, but perhaps you and your family can discuss ways that you might reach out to someone in your school or community who is struggling and serve that person. Together, you and the Lord can decide what it is you might do.

How will you lift?

How might you strengthen?

_____
_____
_____

How could you support?

_____
_____
_____

Do you know someone carrying a burden so heavy that you might help him or her hold on for a time? **Could you journey with that person?**

_____
_____
_____

Remember to keep your purpose in mind: not to solve others' problems, but to bring them closer to Christ. Add your faith to theirs. Pray for them. Serve them. Talk to them about Jesus. Through Him, the miracles will come.

Provide a Refuge for Weary Travelers

THE CONVERSATION
Luke 5:18–20

To what lengths would you go to bring a friend to Christ? How might you lift? Strengthen? Hold on? Support? Could you add your faith to that friend's? Discuss the pure love of Christ. How could your family develop that attribute this month?

THE CONNECTION

Think of someone you know who is struggling right now. Come up with a specific plan that would lift that person's heart. Spend the month focusing on ways you might lift, strengthen, hold on to, or support someone close to you.

THE CELEBRATION

Oven-Baked S'mores

Place 8 to 10 marshmallows on a parchment-lined baking sheet. Place under broiler. Watch constantly and turn marshmallows as soon as they begin to brown. Remove from oven when toasted.

Place in between two graham crackers with chocolate squares.

This is a fun way to make s'mores year round!

THE LESSON FROM THE HOUSE THAT WAS FULL

⟶ ⟶ ⟶

If you seek a household of love, provide a refuge for weary travelers.

THE LORD'S HOUSE

A Household of

Walk with Him

My great-grandfather devoted his life to raising sheep in the high mountains of Coalville, Utah. As part of his legacy, the property he owned for sheepherding in the early 1900s has been handed down from generation to generation in our family. It is a place we love to visit. There is something so peaceful about leaving behind paved asphalt for roads made of dirt and rustic surroundings. I wish you could come for a visit. You would still see flocks of sheep grazing along the mountainside, we would probably sneak up on a mother elk with her young baby down by the fishing pond, and we might even see a moose in the upper meadow. The afternoon would be spent canoeing on the pond and hiking the trails. After dinner we would settle into camp chairs around a crackling fire, and as the evening breeze came through you would hear the soft rustling of aspen leaves in the tall trees. It is one of my favorite places to visit in the entire world.

Last year my husband and brother suggested that our family build a yurt—a structure that looks like a permanent tent of sorts—to provide a refuge from the storms, the heat, and the wildlife on the land. We are not builders by trade, but the yurt company told us they would send us a pattern that would help us know how to proceed.

When the instructions came, the pattern for the foundation was on one sheet of paper. It looked so simple. We took the pattern they sent us and measured it out onto the parcel of land we had chosen. Then we hammered stakes into the ground, pulled strings across the stakes to mark the location for each hole, and proceeded to spend hours and hours digging through rocky terrain to create holes deep enough to pour the foundation. It was a greater adventure than the pattern had alluded to! In fact, it took an entire summer just to lay the foundation right. At each step we checked the pattern and then checked it again. We had been told that if we were careful and diligent with setting the foundation, the rest of the process would be easy.

As we built, I kept thinking of my own home—not in a physical sense, but in a figurative sense. I pondered the foundation we were creating for our family. I tried to focus on the patterns that we were following. I wondered if we were doing enough groundwork to prepare our family for what would lie ahead.

What is the foundation your home is built upon?

This process made me realize that there is a great work to be done and that the best results will come if our spiritual foundation is built upon the teachings of Jesus Christ. I realized that just like building the yurt, creating a Christ-centered home would require deliberate patterns and careful planning.

The choice to become a true follower of Jesus Christ brings with it holy patterns that will define us as a people of Christ. These holy patterns can become the foundation of our homes. Let me explain what I mean.

The choice to become a true follower of Jesus Christ brings with it holy patterns that will define us as a people of Christ.

If we study the Lord's house, or temple, as described in the Old Testament, we discover that it was a house of patterns. First, the house had a wall around it to separate the sanctuary from the common place (see Ezekiel 42:20). Then, the Lord says, "Let them measure the pattern. . . . shew them the form of the house . . . and the goings out . . . and the comings in, . . . and all the forms . . . and all the ordinances . . . and all the laws . . . that they may keep . . . and do them" (Ezekiel 43:10–11). Last, "They shall teach my people the difference between the holy and profane" (Ezekiel 44:23).

The temple patterns outlined in Ezekiel are important patterns that we can model our own homes after today. If we follow these patterns, our homes can become holy places. The first pattern we need to establish in our homes is that of belief centered in Jesus Christ that will separate us from the influences of the world. Second, we should allow His teachings to establish the guidelines, rules, and habits that will define our family both inside and outside of our homes. Last, our families must learn to recognize the difference between the holiness of the Lord and the common expectations of the world. A great power will come when the patterns we choose to implement in our homes are guided by these three principles.

The first pattern is to establish belief. The New Testament does not define a living place for Jesus once His ministry began. However, we do know that He spent much of His time teaching within the synagogues—a place set apart from the world. Such was the case one afternoon in Capernaum. His sermon was powerful, His invitation clear—*believe in me*. On that afternoon the people came seeking Jesus, but the scriptures tell us that after that experience they left and walked no more with Him. Then Jesus asked the Twelve Apostles, "Will ye also go away?"

Simon Peter answered Him, "Lord, to whom shall we go? . . . We believe and are sure that thou art that Christ, the Son of the living God" (John 6:67–69).

Just like the followers of Jesus in the New Testament, we each will face a time when we must sincerely ask ourselves, "Will you also go away?" Life will question our loyalty to the

Lord time and time again. When we find ourselves on shaky ground, to whom shall we go? In the darkest moment of the deepest night, to whom shall we go? In times of doubt, discouragement, or failure, to whom shall we go? When it seems as if all hope is gone, to whom shall we go? When the burden is too heavy, when our reserves are depleted, when the outcome is uncertain, to whom shall we go?

Will we choose Jesus? Will we walk with Him?

The result of that decision has the power to transform our lives, and it comprises the first pattern we must teach in our homes. Jesus is the Christ, the Son of God. He is the rock, the light in the darkness, the hope when hope is gone. He is truth, encouragement, and the power to overcome. He offers to share the yoke, to fill our reservoirs, and to overcome. He is our all in all. Why would we ever choose to walk no more with Him? His invitation to us today is as simple as it was in the synagogue in Capernaum: "Believe in me." And so the challenge is set before us. The decision is clear. We must consciously work to turn our homes into homes that believe.

What patterns in your home help to establish a belief in Jesus Christ?

The second pattern is to allow Christ's teaching to define our families.

Many years ago, my son Josh and I were having a conversation about being spiritually prepared to handle the situations he was facing in the hallways at school. Sometimes standing as a witness of Jesus Christ requires tough decisions and hard conversations. This was one of those times. We turned to the teachings of Paul that talk about wearing the armor of God, found in Ephesians. I had Josh pull out a piece of scratch paper, and he drew the armor on a stick figure as I read each verse. We talked about each of the pieces and its purpose and how each would have been hand crafted to fit the specific needs of the individual. Then I asked Josh a question: "It looks like your warrior is totally prepared for a frontal attack. What happens if the attack comes from behind?"

A look of great concern crossed Josh's face. "I don't know, Mom," he replied. "What will he do?"

We turned to one of my most favorite verses in Isaiah: "Your righteousness shall go before you; the glory of the Lord shall be your rear guard." (Isaiah 58:8, ESV). We decided that our job is to always wear the armor of God and then to remember that the Lord has our back. He is with us. No matter what battle we face, from any direction, He will be there to help. It was a moment when Christ's teaching strengthened our family. Wearing the armor of God became characteristic of our family, because we had come to understand what it meant. In a small way, the word of the Lord had set our family apart from the world.

Consider the guidelines, rules, and habits that are characteristic of your family. **Do these values set your family apart from the world?**

The last pattern is to help our family members recognize the difference between what is holy and what is common. We live at a time when it is easy to take a casual approach to life. This apathy spreads into ethics, relationships, and even worship. We have largely forgotten the importance of guarding that which is sacred. We have forgotten what it is to live holy. Holiness can be found in the moments that are set apart for the Lord. Perhaps these are times of prayer, scripture study, or meditation. What patterns fill your home that would emphasize the holy? **How might you better emphasize these three patterns in your own home?**

The three lessons taught in the house of the Lord are clear: we must establish a household that worships Jesus Christ. That humble worship will define the characteristics of our home and will help us to create a holy place. As we create experiences to strengthen belief, as we focus on teachings that center on Jesus, and as we set aside moments of holiness, we will come to better understand what it means to walk with Him. Then, when life makes us ask, *to whom shall you go?* our choice will be certain.

We will choose Jesus.

Walk with Him

THE CONVERSATION

John 6:66–69

This month, choose to become a home that believes. Take a few minutes to ponder what it looks like to walk no more with Jesus. Then discuss what it looks like to believe in Him. What patterns come from that belief? After your conversation, write out the holy patterns your family has practiced so far this year. How do you separate what takes place in your home from the common things of the world? What are the guidelines that set your family apart as true followers of Jesus Christ? What are some of the holy patterns that your family participates in regularly?

THE CONNECTION

Decide one way that your family will walk with Jesus this month. Have each member of the family write that goal with a permanent marker on the bottom sole of a favorite pair of shoes. Let it become a reminder to walk with Jesus every day.

THE CELEBRATION

Toffee Apple Dip

Mix together until fluffy:

> 1 package cream cheese
> ½ cup brown sugar
> ¼ cup sugar
> 1 teaspoon vanilla

Stir in 1 package of toffee chips. Serve with sliced apples.

You might consider trying pears with this recipe also. This fun treat would be great to snack on as you have your discussion.

THE LESSON FROM
THE HOUSE OF THE LORD

⸎ ⸎ ⸎

*If you seek
a household of worship,
walk with Him.*

THE HOUSE OF
MARTHA AND MARY

A Household of

Gratitude

Words Cannot Express

Many years ago I received a phone call from a frantic father standing in an airport half the world away.

His daughter, who lived down the street from me, was critically ill. An emergency trip to the hospital was needed. It would take him over fifteen hours to fly home, so his wife would have to go alone to the hospital with the sick toddler and a newborn who could not be left behind. His plea consisted of three words: "Can you go?"

I remember rushing over to their home. Helping pack diaper bags and overnight bags. Trying to find matching shoes. Thinking through the details so that this mother wouldn't have to. I followed her to the hospital and I stayed, while doctors came and went and we were moved from room to room and then floor to floor. I remember the hours of waiting for the woman's husband to fly across the world to be there and the relief that flooded over her face when he finally walked in.

It was several weeks later, after the daughter was healthy again, that her mother stopped by with a plate of cookies and a thank-you note. I still have the note. I keep it in a

drawer in my bedroom, the one where I keep everything
I never want to forget. The card consisted of one simple
line: "There are no words expressive enough to convey my
gratitude."

I cried.

Because I remembered my own heart many years before
as I walked into a hospital room with a deathly ill three-
year-old hanging limp over one shoulder and a ten-month-
old in a car seat grasped firmly in my other hand. I was
alone. I had nothing with me. No overnight bag. No one
to sit with me in those first minutes as doctor after doctor
came in to assess the situation and I waited for my husband
to arrive.

And then my mom walked in the room.

My gratitude was instant and indescribable—the kind of
gratitude that words cannot express.

There have been other moments in my life when I have
felt the profound gratitude this woman had penned on the
thank-you card. Most of them have one thing in common:
they have been moments of great need. Times when I have
not had the strength to face the situation at hand and someone has come to help shoulder the burden. In those moments, there are no words. These experiences remind me of
a story found in the twelfth chapter of John.

It wasn't what the woman said; it was what she did.
That night, after supper, Mary took a pound of ointment
and anointed the feet of Jesus, wiping his feet with her hair.
When she had finished, the house was filled with the fragrance of the ointment. Her act of gratitude did not go

unnoticed. It was Judas who complained. Judas, the thief. Judas, who would betray the Lord. He questioned the purpose of the service. Couldn't the expensive ointment be sold and the money given to the poor? Jesus replied, "Let her alone: against the day of my burying hath she kept this. For the poor always ye have with you; but me ye have not always" (John 12:7–8).

Just like a fragrance, gratitude lingers upon all who come in contact with it, leaving a noticeable sweetness.

Through this story we see so clearly the difference between a disciple and a doubter. It is compelling how the qualities these two people possessed completely determined their actions. Judas had a heart filled with resentment, entitlement, and self-gratification. Mary had a heart filled with sweetness, humility, and gratitude. I don't think it is a coincidence that John tells us the entire house filled with the fragrance of Mary's actions. Just like a fragrance, gratitude lingers upon all who come in contact with it, leaving a noticeable sweetness. Often gratitude is best expressed not with words, but with actions.

When have you seen this to be true?

_____

_____

_____

I attend a weekly Bible study with a group of women I deeply admire. We were recently studying the New Testament—specifically, the subject of commandments. Our group leader asked us what motivated us individually to keep the commandments. It was an intense conversation. We talked of the delicate balance that comes from obedience out of fear and obedience out of love. If we are not

If gratitude is the motivating force behind why we keep God's commandments, our obedience will be based upon love.

careful, we can accidentally turn God into a scorekeeper, which is not His nature. Our group leader asked us what the motivation should be behind our commandment keeping. Without hesitation one woman spoke up: "gratitude," she said simply. "If gratitude is the motivating force behind why we keep God's commandments, our obedience will be based upon love."

I carried that thought with me for many days after that

study. Every time I encountered an opportunity to keep a commandment, I questioned my intentions. Was I about to keep that commandment with a heart filled with gratitude? I thought about it each time I prayed, when I turned to the scriptures, as I attended church. There were opportunities to serve, to teach, to minister, and I tried to approach each with a spirit of gratitude. A remarkable change began to take place in my heart; I felt an increase in my capacity to love those I was with. But more importantly, I felt an increase in my love for God.

Mary had kept that box of ointment for a special purpose. She kept it in preparation for the Savior's death. She used it to express her gratitude for the unspeakable gift He was about to offer her. Her actions were motivated by sweetness, humility, and gratitude. Perhaps our gratitude to God is best expressed through action rather than words. When our actions become the expression of our gratitude, then our time, our sacrifice, and our obedience become gifts rather than duties.

Is there one commandment you could approach with a heart full of gratitude this month? **How would gratitude change the way you keep that commandment?**

_____

_____

_____

Many years ago we opened our home to a teenage boy who was struggling. He was failing school, vandalizing the neighborhood on a regular basis, and involved with drugs.

He had a learning disability that made it impossible for him to do homework on his own and a family situation that did not provide help. So we invited this boy several nights a week for dinner and homework help in the evenings. Soon there were other neighbors who wanted to help out, and eventually this boy had dinner and homework help provided every single night of the week. One evening we gathered as a family to have a counsel and discussion on gratitude. It was November, and I wanted to set a goal for our family to consider ways we might be more grateful all month long. I handed each person a piece of paper and asked everyone to answer three questions: Who is one person in your life who has served you? What did that person sacrifice? What can you learn about serving from that person's example? Then I was going to have all the members of the family write a thank-you note to the person they had thought of. Immediately everyone started writing. Everyone except Garett, the boy who visited our home for dinner and homework help. I went over and sat on the couch next to him and asked quietly, "Do you need help deciding what to write?"

"No," he answered quickly. "I know what I want to write about. I want to write about the families who take me in for dinner and homework help every night. I just don't have words."

Now that boy lives with us. He loves to mow my lawn, detail my car, take out my garbage. Most of the time I don't even have to ask him; he sees a need and he immediately fulfills it. When my husband asks him about it, the way he does things around the house without being asked, he always replies, "It's the least I can do for being able to live here." His actions demonstrate his gratitude. He is one of the most gracious people I know.

My favorite people in the world all have one thing in common: they are filled with gratitude. It is almost as if they can't contain it; it spills out of them continuously.

Do you know someone like that? How would you describe that person?

_____

_____

_____

I want to become more filled with gratitude. I want my children to be filled to overflowing with that characteristic. This month, I want to work on ways that we can express our gratitude with not only words but also with actions within our home, in our community, and with God.

Maybe this month, we could focus on performing our assigned household duties as a gift rather than as a chore. We could try to express gratitude to one family member before bed each day. We could look for ways to reach out with gratitude in our community. Our prayers could be filled with giving thanks rather than asking. Our daily religious tasks could become less of a checklist of duties and more of an offering of gratitude.

Words Cannot Express

THE CONVERSATION

John 12:3-8

Try to think of the most gracious person you know. How does this person express gratitude? What part do you think gratitude plays in keeping the commandments of God?

THE CONNECTION

Take some time to create a gratitude poster to hang in your home. Put it in an area where family members will frequently walk past it. Leave a marker nearby. Encourage the members of your family to write down something they are grateful for every single time they walk by. You will be amazed at how much joy will come from reading the thoughts on the poster throughout the month.

THE CELEBRATION

Coconut Rice Crispy Squares

1 bag of marshmallows (10 ounces)
5 cups crisped rice cereal
½ cup coconut oil

Melt marshmallows and coconut oil in microwave for three minutes. Stir mixture together until smooth. Add crisped rice cereal and stir until combined. Pour into glass dish and flatten top. Cut into bars and serve.

You think you love butter in this familiar recipe, but just wait until you try coconut oil. These treats will never be the same again!

THE LESSON FROM THE HOUSE OF MARTHA AND MARY

🌱 🌱 🌱

If you seek a household of gratitude, let actions portray what words cannot express.

THE HOUSE
ON THE ROCK

A Household

Built upon Christ

Build upon a Rock

I am one who is immensely intrigued by the Amish faith. It has been my opportunity many times to drive through the back roads of several states the Amish people call home. I drive slowly when I am there. I take in the simplicity of their homesteads, I admire the handcrafting of their buggies, I stop time and time again in the little markets that house their hand-stitched quilts. My library contains several books describing the rustic and simple life of the Amish. Their way of living calls to my heart.

I am not alone in my intrigue with the Amish. Many years ago an Amish newspaper ran a story describing the hundreds of letters they received from people who wanted to know how to become Amish. Usually these people were seeking stillness from living a hurried life. They thought becoming Amish would provide a solution. "Uncle Amos," an Amish man who wrote for the *Small Farmer's Journal,* penned this response: "Many non-Amish wish they had our values but are not willing to work at acquiring and keeping them. They think we are what we are because of our way of life . . . but the truth is we live our way of life because of what we are. We realize not everyone is cut out to be one of the plain people. Many have not the opportunity; but here is the challenge: If you admire our faith, strengthen yours. If you admire our sense of commitment, deepen yours. If you admire our community spirit, build your own. If you admire our simple life, cut back. If you admire deep character and enduring values, live them yourself" (Uncle Amos, *Small Farmer's Journal* [Vol. 17, No. 3], 43).

His sentiment reminds me of the teaching of Jesus when He gave the Sermon on the Mount. You remember the teaching style Jesus uses—if anyone asks for your tunic, let him have your cloak; if anyone asks you to go one mile, go with him two; if someone slaps you on the right cheek, turn to him the other. He was teaching the higher law, the law of a true Christian. Don't just serve; serve like *this*. Don't just fast; fast like *this*. Don't just pray; pray like *this*. At the end of the sermon, Jesus spoke of two gates and two walkways, two trees and two houses. You could choose between a strait gate and a narrow path or a wide gate and broad path. There was a tree that brought forth good fruit or a tree that brought forth evil fruit. And after the gate, and the path, and the tree, there was a house, and again, a choice. You could choose the house built upon sand or the house built upon a rock. "And the rain descended, and the floods came, and the winds blew, and beat upon that house; and it fell not: for it was founded upon a rock" (Matthew 7:25).

In all my days, I have never witnessed a house built on top of a rock. Because of that, I have often wondered what was meant by this verse. One day when I was reading in the book of Samuel, the answer came: "The Lord is my rock, and my fortress, and my deliverer" (2 Samuel 22:2). Jesus Christ is the rock. We must build our houses upon Him. Then we will find ourselves opening the strait gate, walking down the narrow path that leads under the tree that brings forth good fruit, and entering a home founded upon Him, upon His teachings, upon His word. More than anything, I want to live in a home like that. The early Saints understood this principle; they based their way of life around it: "In every house, they ceased not to teach and preach Jesus Christ" (Acts 5:42). Perhaps the same could be true today.

When Christ becomes the center of our home, our way of living begins to define us as true Christians—we live our way of life because of who we are.

Sometimes when I get to the last chapter of a book I like to look back through all of the other chapters and remember what I have learned. This journey has allowed us a deeper look into some of the homes Jesus visited. We discovered principles and patterns that can change our own homes if we continue to work at acquiring and keeping them. We have learned that when Christ becomes the center of our home, our way of living begins to define us as true Christians—we live our way of life because of who we are. The scriptures tell us that not everyone will choose this way of life. Some may not have the opportunity. But for those of us who do, here is the invitation:

If you seek a household where He abides,
invite Him in.

If you seek a household of faith,
expect miracles.

If you seek a household of prayer,
converse with Him.

If you seek a household of scripture,
embrace the stories of Jesus.

If you seek a household of holiness,
honor the day that is His.

If you seek a household of unity,
do nice and be sweet.

If you seek a household of grace,
discover it in the ordinary.

If you seek a household of change,
forget your perfect offering.

If you seek a household of love,
provide a refuge for weary travelers.

If you seek a household of worship,
walk with Him.

If you seek a household of gratitude,
let actions portray what words cannot express.

If you seek a household built upon a rock,
make Christ the center of your home.

⌃ ⌃ ⌃

Build Your House upon the Rock

THE CONVERSATION

Matthew 7:24–25

What would it look like if you were to build your home upon the rock of Jesus Christ?

THE CONNECTION

Spend some time discussing each of the households above. Can you remember the lessons from every month? What were some of your favorites? Which principles and patterns have become a permanent part of your home? Are there one or two lessons you would like to study again? **What are your thoughts?**

_____

_____

_____

THE CELEBRATION

Laurel's Bananas Foster

1 stick butter
½ cup brown sugar
⅓ cup corn syrup
1 capful coconut oil
4 bananas
Coconut chocolate chip ice cream

Boil butter, sugar, and corn syrup for two minutes. Add coconut oil.

Slice four bananas and put them into the caramel mixture.

Scoop coconut chocolate chip ice cream into bowls and pour the bananas foster syrup over the top.

Most people pour the caramel syrup over vanilla ice cream—not Laurel. Her recipe just might become one of your new favorites.

THE LESSON FROM THE HOUSE ON THE ROCK

🌿 🌿 🌿

If you seek a household built upon a rock, make Christ the center of your home.

Acknowledgments

The end of every writing process always leaves me with a grateful heart. To those gifted with the ability to take words on a page and weave them into a life-changing experience, I express my deepest gratitude. Richard Erickson, Sheryl Dickert Smith, Barry Hansen, and Rachael Ward, your unending patience with this endeavor allowed this manuscript to become what I hoped and envisioned it might be—heartfelt thanks to each of you. Tracy Keck, you wear so many different hats so beautifully. Thank you for being editor, designer, and visionary all wrapped up in one. Your enthusiasm for this project once again reminded me why I love to write. Chris Schoebinger, Lisa Mangum, and all the others who work endlessly behind the scenes at Ensign Peak, thank you for believing in this journey that few have traveled before us and for constantly looking for ways to help us move one more small step forward. To Laurel Day, who championed this cause from the very first, and Chrislyn Woolston, who has been the greatest cheerleader anyone could ever ask for, thank you for your words of wisdom and your words of encouragement depending on the day. Both were so needed, and so appreciated. Deepest gratitude to Lysa Terkeurst who once reminded me that God will make divine appointments for us, and we must be brave enough to keep them. It is a lesson I won't forget. And last, to Greg. You are my best critic, my greatest support, and my most favorite part of every journey. Thanks for walking beside me these last twenty-six years.

About the Author

Emily Belle Freeman is a coach's wife, mother to five children and a few others who have found refuge in her home, author of several bestselling books, and sought-after inspirational speaker. Her days are spent watching over teenagers, her flock of pampered chickens, and two rabbits that she adores. She finds great joy in studying the life and teachings of Jesus Christ. Her deep love of the scriptures comes from a desire to find their application in everyday life.

For a few minutes every day Emily forgets about laundry, leaves the dishes in the sink, and writes. She coauthors a blog that is a stopping place for hearts seeking all that is good: www.multiplygoodness.com.